Foul Deeds and Suspicious Deaths In Barking, Dagenham & Chadwell Heath

FOUL DEEDS AND SUSPICIOUS DEATHS Series

Wharncliffe's *Foul Deeds and Suspicious Deaths* series explores, in detail, crimes of passion, brutal murders and foul misdemeanours from early modern times to the present day. Victorian street crime, mysterious death and modern murders tell tales where passion, jealousy and social deprivation brought unexpected violence to those involved. From unexplained death and suicide to murder and manslaughter, the books provide a fascinating insight into the lives of both victims and perpetrators as well as society as a whole.

Other titles in the series include:

Foul Deeds and Suspicious Deaths in Birmingham, Nick Billingham
ISBN: 1-903425-96-4. £10.99
Foul Deeds and Suspicious Deaths Around the Black Country,
David John Cox and Michael Pearson
ISBN: 1-845630-0-41. £10.99
Foul Deeds and Suspicious Deaths in and around Bradford, Stephen Wade
ISBN: 1-903425-83-2. £10.99
Foul Deeds and Suspicious Deaths in and around Bristol, Veronica Smith
ISBN: 1-845630-13-0. £10.99
Foul Deeds and Suspicious Deaths in and around Carlisle, Ian Ashbridge
ISBN: 1-845630-1-57. £10.99
Foul Deeds and Suspicious Deaths in Colchester, Patrick Denney
ISBN: 1-903425-80-8. £10.99
Foul Deeds and Suspicious Deaths in Croydon, Caroline Maxton
ISBN: 1-845630-0-76. £10.99
Foul Deeds and Suspicious Deaths Around Derby, Kevin Turton
ISBN: 1-903425-76-X. £9.99
Foul Deeds and Suspicious Deaths in and around Durham, Maureen Anderson
ISBN: 1-903425-46-8. £9.99
Foul Deeds and Suspicious Deaths in Ealing, Dr Jonathan Oates
ISBN: 1-845630-1-22. £12.99
Foul Deeds and Suspicious Deaths in London's East End, Geoffrey Howse
ISBN: 1-903425-71-9. £10.99
Foul Deeds and Suspicious Deaths in Guernsey, Glynis Cooper
ISBN: 1-845630-0-84. £10.99
Foul Deeds and Suspicious Deaths in Hampstead, Holborn & St Pancras,
Mark Aston
ISBN: 1-903425-94-8. £10.99
Foul Deeds and Suspicious Deaths in Hull, David Goodman
ISBN: 1-903425-43-3. £9.99
Foul Deeds and Suspicious Deaths in Manchester, Martin Baggoley
ISBN: 1-903425-65-4. £9.99
Foul Deeds and Suspicious Deaths in Newport, Terry Underwood
ISBN: 1-903425-59-X. £9.99
Foul Deeds and Suspicious Deaths on the Yorkshire Coast, Alan Whitworth
ISBN: 1-903425-01-8. £9.99

Foul Deeds & Suspicious Deaths in
Barking, Dagenham & Chadwell Heath

Linda Rhodes & Kathryn Abnett

Series Editor
Brian Elliott

Wharncliffe Books

First Published in Great Britain in 2007 by
Wharncliffe Books
an imprint of
Pen and Sword Books Limited,
47 Church Street, Barnsley,
South Yorkshire. S70 2AS

ISBN: 978 1 84563 034 8

A CIP catalogue record of this book is available from the
British Library

Typeset in Plantin and Benguiat by
Pen and Sword Books Ltd

Printed in the United Kingdom by
CPI UK

Pen & Sword Books Ltd incorporates the imprints of
Pen & Sword Aviation, Pen & Sword Maritime,
Pen & Sword Military, Wharncliffe Local History, Pen & Sword Select,
Pen & Sword Military Classics and Leo Cooper.

For a complete list of Pen & Sword titles please contact:
PEN & SWORD BOOKS LIMITED
47 Church Street, Barnsley, South Yorkshire, S70 2AS, England.
E-mail: enquiries@pen-and-sword.co.uk
Website: www.pen-and-sword.co.uk

Contents

Acknowledgements

We would like to thank the following for their generous assistance:

Tahlia Coombs, Ian Dowling, Judith Etherton, Jeff Ewbank, Clive Gowlett, Ann and Pieter Ketting, Peter Midlane, Ron and Joyce Petchey, Lee Shelden, Roy Shoesmith, Derek Simmans and Mark Watson.

Grateful acknowledgements are also due to the Revd Gordon Tarry and the churchwardens of St Margaret's Church, Barking, for the use of photographs of the church interior.

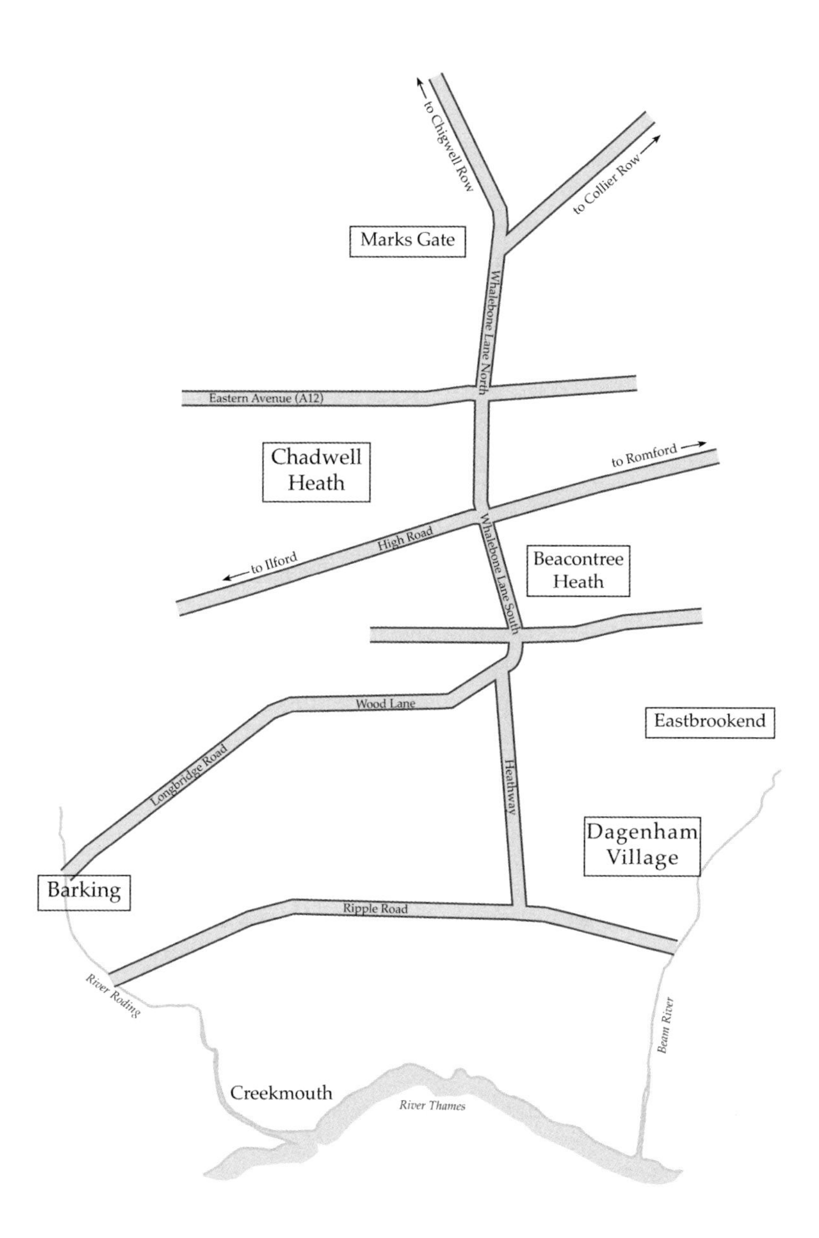

Location map of places featured in this book

Introduction

Barking and Dagenham can trace their names back to Saxon times, Barking meaning 'Berica's people' and Dagenham 'Daecca's home'. The area now covered by Barking, Dagenham and Chadwell Heath once formed part of the Barking Abbey estates. According to legend the Abbey, founded around the year 666 by St Erkenwald, was the scene of one of the foulest deeds that can be imagined. The marauding Vikings are said to have destroyed the Abbey buildings, stolen its treasures and killed its inhabitants. It is easy to imagine the longships creeping silently up the River Roding in the early morning mist, with fearsome warriors in horned helmets waiting to leap out and wreak death and destruction. Historians, though, are sceptical that a massacre actually took place, and also cast scorn on the horned helmets!

The stories that follow, however, are all true. They describe dramatic and often disturbing events in the area's history up to the mid-twentieth century. Many accounts of gruesome murders, particularly in Dagenham and Chadwell Heath, are published here for the first time. There are also descriptions of disasters, both natural and man-made, which reflect the history of Barking as an important fishing port and industrial centre.

Barking Abbey as it may have looked in the year 1500. LBBD Archives at Valence House Museum

Chapter 1

Martyrs, Witches, Plotters, Pirates, Highwaymen and Bodysnatchers

... a shot was fired, and a voice shouted, 'By God we have got him!'

Burned at the stake

In mid-1550s England, people who refused to conform with the religion of the monarch risked losing their lives. On succeeding her Protestant brother, Edward VI, Queen Mary reinstated Roman Catholicism. Among those persecuted for continuing to follow the Protestant faith were Christopher Lyster from Dagenham and Hugh Laverock of Barking, whose stories are told in John Foxe's *Book of Martyrs.*

Christopher Lyster

In spring 1556 Christopher Lyster, a blind farmer, was sent to Colchester prison for refusing to attend his parish church. From there he and five other men were brought before the Bishop of London, at Fulham Palace, to be interrogated about their beliefs. They agreed that they had spoken against the authority of the Pope, describing him as 'an oppressor of Christ's church and gospel', and saying that he should have no power in England. Christopher Lyster also declared that the Mass was 'mere idolatry and abomination'. Attempts were made to persuade them to renounce their faith, but the men refused to comply, and were condemned to death. On 28 April 1556 they were burned at the stake at Colchester. Their names are listed on a memorial on the south wall inside St Peter's Church in that town.

Hugh Laverock

Three days after the death of Christopher Lyster, 68 year old Hugh Laverock, a painter, was also brought before the Bishop on the same charge. He was questioned along with John Apprice, a blind man, and the pair robustly defended their beliefs. They were sent to Newgate Prison, and on 9 May 1556 appeared before the Consistory Court of St Paul's and were asked whether they would recant. Hugh Laverock, referring to the Mass, replied 'I cannot find in the Scriptures, that the priests should lift up over their head a cake of bread'. They were condemned to be burned to death at the stake. Six days later, on 15 May 1556, the two men were taken in a cart from Newgate to Stratford-le-Bow to be executed. After being chained to the stake, Hugh Laverock, who was very lame, threw away his crutch, saying to John Apprice, 'Be of good cheer my brother; for my lord of London is a good physician; he will heal us both shortly – thee of thy blindness, and me of my lameness'. Their names appear on a memorial at Stratford.

Witches

During the next reign, that of Elizabeth I, the death penalty for witchcraft was re-introduced. James Howson, in his article *Brooms at Midnight*, writes that 'it was the poor, usually old and unprotected, who were most frequently accused in England'. Two Barking and two Dagenham women were among the hundreds convicted and hanged.

Cicely Glasenbury

In 1574 Cicely, the wife of a Barking yeoman named Thomas Glasenbury, and also known as Mother Arnold, faced a number of accusations. A pamphlet of 1595 described how she allegedly bewitched Thomas Clark, a Barking fisherman. While out in his boat he suddenly cried out that he could see Mother Arnold 'walking in the water'. He felt her spirit attempting to make him kill himself, so he threw overboard a hatchet, a hook and a knife. He then tied himself to the mast as he was afraid he would jump into the water. Taken back to Barking, 'he remained mad and in the end dyed thus tormented'. Cicely Glasenbury, accused of causing Clark's death, was examined by magistrate Clement Sysley at Eastbury House. As Sysley was writing out the warrant to commit her to prison, 'suddenly both his feete were taken from him by reason whereof he fell on a plain pavement of free stone in his own house'. The fall dislocated his thigh-bone. At the Essex Assizes in July 1574 Cicely was also accused of causing the deaths of John Fyssher, Giles Graye, William Gyleet and a grey gelding, as well as serious injury to William Newman. She was found guilty on all counts, sentenced to death, and hanged at Barking. For three weeks after her execution, Clement Sysley was still forced to use crutches.

Elizabeth Harding

Another Barking woman, Elizabeth Harding, was charged in August 1579 with causing the death by witchcraft of 3 year old Cecily Miles. She was also accused of bewitching to death twelve horses worth £30 belonging to Michael Towler, and of causing great injury to Ellen, wife of John Goode. At first Elizabeth Harding was found not guilty of Cecily's death, and sentenced to a year's imprisonment on the other charges. While still in prison at Colchester, in March 1580 she was again charged with the death of Cecily Miles. This time there was a guilty verdict, and she was hanged at Colchester.

Joan Upney

Some Dagenham women were also denounced as witches. Joan Upney, for example, was brought before magistrate Sir Henry Grey of Pirgo, near Romford, on 3 May 1589. Witches were often believed to have assistance from 'familiars', demons in the guise of cats, dogs, ravens and other creatures. Joan confessed that she had used toads to kill the wives of two men who had previously accused her of witchcraft. Apparently she had left one at the house of John Harrolde, and it pinched his wife Joan and 'sucked her till she dyed'. Another toad had pinched Alice, the wife of Richard Foster, causing her death. Joan Upney was put on trial, found guilty and hanged at Chelmsford along with Joan Prentice and Joan Cony on 5 July 1589.

The hanging of Joan Upney and two others in 1589. LBBD Archives at Valence House Museum

A contemporary pamphlet records that on the scaffold

> *Mother Upney…cryed out saying: that she had greevously sinned, that the devill had deceived her…that she had twice given her soule to the Devill…she seemed very sorry for ye same, and died very penitent, asking God & the world forgivenes, even to ye last gaspe, for her wicked and detestable life.*

Ellen Gray

Two years later, in 1591, Joan Upney's accusers John Harrolde and Richard Foster denounced another Dagenham woman. Ellen (or Helen) Gray faced five charges: bewitching Anne Bixon, 'of which she died', 'Richard Foster in his body', 'a cow worth 32s 4d belonging to Henry Whood so that it died', 'Ellen Playt, whereby she languished', and 'foure gallon of creame belonging to John Harrolde, so that butter could not be made of it'. Ellen was found guilty of all charges and hanged.

Eastbury House and the Gunpowder Plot

In 1605 a group of Catholic conspirators wishing to overthrow the Establishment planted barrels of gunpowder in the vaults below the House of Lords, intending to detonate them on 5 November when King James I opened Parliament. Their scheme was foiled after an anonymous letter of warning was sent to Lord Monteagle. Local legend has always linked Eastbury House in Barking with the Gunpowder Plot, but can this be proved?

A romantic view of Eastbury House from an old postcard. Authors' collection

Eastbury was built in the mid-sixteenth century and is situated just south of Ripple Road on what was formerly an expanse of open marshland looking across to the Thames. In the 1720s Daniel Defoe described it as 'a great house, antient, and now almost fallen down, where tradition says the Gunpowder Treason Plot was at first contriv'd, and that all the first consultations about it were held there'. Daniel Lysons, in his *Environs of London* (1796) added rumours of another connection: 'There is tradition relating to this house, either, as some say, that the conspirators who concerted the gunpowder plot held their meetings there, or as others, that it was the residence of Lord Monteagle, when he received the letter which led to the discovery'. Lysons noted, however, that these legends were 'both, perhaps, equally destitute of foundation'.

In 1872 T.E.C. Streatfeild, in a lecture to the Royal Institute of British Architects, said that 'It is worth noticing, however, that to this day excursionists, on their way to Rosherville and Southend, point to Eastbury as "Guy Fawkes" house'. Streatfeild dismissed this as 'mythical', but was convinced that at the time of the Gunpowder Plot Lord Monteagle himself was renting Eastbury House from the owner, Mrs Steward. Monteagle had formerly been enthusiastic for the Catholic cause, and had even been imprisoned in the Tower during Elizabeth's reign. The registers of St Margaret's Church, Barking, reveal that Monteagle's son William was baptized there on 3 December 1607. Mrs Steward was known to be living elsewhere, and as 'the inhabitants of the other manor houses can be accounted for' Streatfeild concluded that Lord Monteagle did reside at Eastbury.

On 9 November 1605, just four days after Guy Fawkes was arrested in the Parliament cellars, investigations linked him to Barking. State Papers reveal that Sir Nicholas Coote, a magistrate living at Valence House, in Dagenham, interrogated a Barking fisherman named Richard Franklin. It seemed that Franklin's master, Henry Parish, had hired out a boat to Fawkes (who was using the alias Johnson) so that Fawkes and another man could travel in disguise from Barking to the French port of Gravelines. On returning to England the pair allegedly arranged that after the explosion they were to be conveyed back to France. Franklin also said that Henry Parish had transported Catholic priests to Calais.

In spite of this evidence, the second volume of the *Victoria County History of Essex*, (1907) was entirely sceptical, declaring 'There is no foundation for the legendary connexion of Eastbury House with the Plot'. So the matter rested until the end of the twentieth century, when new evidence came to light to back up the local legend. The *Ilford Herald* of 22 October 1999 ran the headline 'Gunpowder Intrigue: the plot thickens – new discovery links Eastbury Manor to treason'. The article began:

Persistent rumours that Eastbury Manor House in Barking was connected to the infamous 17th century Gunpowder Plot may be based on fact, after all. With only a fortnight to go before Bonfire Night, Barking and

Dagenham's Heritage Officer Mark Watson has announced his discovery of definite links between the house in Eastbury Square and two of the conspirators.

Mr Watson had found in the National Archives an inventory of goods belonging to Alderman John Moore on his death in 1603. It showed that Moore's Spanish Catholic widow, Maria, her daughter Maria Perez and son-in-law Lewis Tresham were living at Eastbury at that time. Lewis was the brother of Francis Tresham and cousin of Robert Catesby, two conspirators executed for their part in the plot. Lewis was also the brother-in-law of Lord Monteagle. It appears that Mrs Moore and her family lived at Eastbury until at least 1606. Mark Watson told the newspaper: 'It is the strongest evidence we have ever found of the link with the plot. It now seems the conspirators may really have met at Eastbury'.

Sold into slavery

From medieval times fishing was the chief industry of Barking. The town's fishermen were often pressed into service with the Navy, and their boats used as additions to the naval fleet. In the 1600s vessels sailing in the Atlantic and Mediterranean were at constant risk of attack from the 'Barbary Pirates', who came from North African ports such as Algiers and Tunis but were also known as 'Turks' because their homeland was at that time part of the Turkish Empire. One of the main aims of these pirates was to take captives and sell them into slavery. Thousands of prisoners were taken in the first half of the seventeenth century. Many people, such as Sir James Cambell of Barking, left money in their wills for the release of 'Turkish captives'.

The fishermen's window at St Margaret's Church, Barking, designed by George Jack.

One such unfortunate was John Anderson, a former Barking fisherman on board a Navy ship travelling from the Bay of Biscay to London that was ambushed by the pirates. He was taken to the port of Sallee in Morocco and sold as a slave for 80 ducats. Anderson wrote to his father Thomas, also a Barking fisherman, that he would be set free if a ransom of £80 was paid. It was impossible for Thomas Anderson, a poor man with a large family, to raise this sum, so he sought permission at the Essex Quarter Sessions in September 1646 for a licence to collect funds from sympathizers throughout the county.

His petition was signed by the vicar and churchwardens of Barking as well as many parishioners. He wrote that his son was 'indureinge that miserable slavery and bondage that it is impossible for Pen to write or Tongue expresse' and 'the which if he faile of the poore Captive is like utterly to perish'. The magistrates at the assizes approved the petition, and according to F.G. Emmison, Essex County Archivist, the ransom money was duly raised and John Anderson set free.

A Visit from Dick Turpin and his Gang

Longbridge Farm

In the winter of 1734 England's most famous highwayman turned his attention to Barking. At about 7 p.m. on the evening of Thursday, 19 December 73 year old Ambrose Skinner of Longbridge Farm was about to lock the front door when, as he later described in a sworn statement: 'Six Armed Men unknown to this Informant with their Faces Muffled and Disguised Rushed in upon him with violence and presenting their Carabines to his Breast swore if he made any Noise or Resistance, they would immediately put him to Death'.

Skinner's hands were bound with his own garters, and he was forced to take Turpin and his fellow raiders from room to room and show them where his valuables were kept. They tried unsuccessfully to unlock the chests and trunks, then broke them open. Altogether they stole more than £47 in cash plus plate, goods, linen and clothing worth approximately £300. Skinner's statement continued:

> *the Said Armed Men continued in his said dwelling House, rifling the same, near the Space of three Hours and an half, after which having taken two Horses out of his Stable to ennable them to carry off their Spoil, they departed; and as this Informant hath been since credebly informed, were seen to pass with others in their Company part on foot and part on Horseback thro the Town of Barking aforesaid, and also thro some of the Turnpikes in the High Road from Essex to London.*

The only other person in the house when the robbers first entered was 21 year old servant Elizabeth King, whom they locked in an upstairs room.

Dick Turpin in his Epping Forest lair. LBBD Archives at Valence House Museum

Two of the male farm servants arrived shortly afterwards only to be ambushed and tied up. Skinner's 35 year old son, also named Ambrose, and daughter-in-law came in at about 8 p.m. and received the same treatment. Skinner junior later stated that the robbers left the family with no clothes apart from those they were wearing.

Dick Turpin was in fact a far cry from the image of the dashing, handsome highwayman. A reward poster of February 1735 described him as 'a fresh-coloured man, very much marked with the small pox, about five feet nine inches high...wears a blue coat and a light-coloured wig'.

Longbridge Farm, scene of the daring raid, was situated where the Barking campus of the University of East London later stood.

Hainault Lodge

Two days later, in the evening of Saturday, 21 December 1734, a gang of at least six men attacked Hainault Lodge, near the northern edge of the parish of Dagenham. It was the house of the warden of Hainault Forest, William Mason, whose duty was to ensure that the forest laws were obeyed and that poachers were apprehended.

At about six p.m. Mason's 13 year old daughter answered a knock at the door, and a man asked if her father was at home. She answered that he was, and when a male servant went to the door, a shot was fired, and a voice shouted 'By God we have got him!' Luckily for the man, mistaken for his master, the shot missed. It appears that William Mason was targeted because he was a zealous prosecutor of deer stealers.

Mason stated that the robbers, with faces covered, burst into the house and fired more shots at him. He, his wife and daughter managed to escape, leaving behind a servant girl and William Roades, Mrs Mason's 68 year old uncle. The intruders forced the elderly man to give them candles so that they could search the house. They ransacked it and took away £140 in cash, nine silver spoons, twelve guns and all or most of Mrs Mason's clothes. It was later claimed that Dick Turpin himself was not present at this raid, but was given a share of the booty. Turpin was eventually convicted of horse-stealing and executed at York in April 1739.

A Grave Offence

Bodysnatchers, also known as Resurrectionists or Resurrection Men, would dig up coffins of newly-buried people, break them open and sell the corpses to surgical and medical schools for dissection. The practice began in the last quarter of the eighteenth century and flourished until the passing of the *Anatomy Act* in 1832. William Holmes Frogley, a Barking fisherman's son who, in the late nineteenth and early twentieth century, wrote an informal history of the town, stated that he 'has been told of several instances of bodysnatching taking place at Barking, by old inhabitants'. Frogley wrote that about sixty years before his time, a gang of seven or eight men in Barking were actually earning their living by bodysnatching. He went on: 'They worked at Barking, East Ham and Little Ilford and in those days, when anyone was buried, it was usual to watch the grave for some days.' Frogley gives the example of a Mrs Kingshott who was buried in East

Ham in the late 1820s. Her husband was warned that an attempt would be made to remove her body:

> *Accordingly he put eight men to watch and about 9 o'clock at night three men appeared, went to the grave and commenced to dig. Out rushed the watchers and caught the three, bound them with ropes and dragged them backwards and forwards through a pond close by in East Ham...They were afterwards taken to Barking Gaol and later sentenced to a term of imprisonment.*

John Hughes, a Barking slopseller (dealer in cheap, ready-made clothing), believed that he had a foolproof method of foiling the bodysnatchers. On 10 November 1823 he registered his invention at the Patent Office under the title *Securing bodies in coffins*. His idea was to add an extra bottom to the coffin and fasten the body to it, then attach a metal grating to cover the whole corpse. His detailed description of the fastenings included:

> *a collar or strap to be put on the neck of the corpse... two straps, the one end of each to go through the holes in the neck strap to be secured to the extra bottom of the coffin with nuts or screws on the undermost side. The other ends of these straps are to go under the arms of the corpse...a number of straps riveted or welded together to form a grating or cage to cover the corpse from head to foot, and fastened to the extra bottom or bottoms, or to the sides of the coffin, with nuts and screws... .*

It is not known whether this device was ever used. If it was, did it succeed in defeating the bodysnatchers?

Sources

Gibson, Marion: *Early modern witches: witchcraft cases in contemporary writing* (2000)

Howson, James: Brooms at midnight (in *Recording the past*, compiled and edited by Alan Hill and Susan Curtis, 1996)

Green, Georgina & Lockwood, Herbert Hope: Is there any truth in the stories linking Eastbury House with the Gunpowder Plot? (*Newsletter of the Barking & District Historical Society*, December 2000)

Rodger, N.A.M: *The safeguard of the sea: a naval history of Britain*, 666-1649 (1997)

Statement of Ambrose Skinner (National Archives, SP 36/33 folios 142-143)

Foxe's book of martyrs is on the Internet at: http://www.hrionline.ac.uk/johnfoxe

Frogley, W.H: *Mr Frogley's Barking, a second selection* (edited by Tony Clifford & Herbert Hope Lockwood, 2002)

Chapter 2

Robbery at the Whalebones

The dog was lying by the side of the chest, dead. It had been given food laced with prussic acid.

Chadwell Heath High Road lies along the ancient route from London to Colchester. John Peter Shawcross noted in his *History of Dagenham* that this section of the busy road was a notorious haunt of highwaymen:

> *Many a coach was stopped and robbed by the 'gentlemen of the road', with crape-covered faces and pistols in holsters. Many a lonely pedestrian had cause to treasure in his breast unpleasant memories of Chadwell Heath. No wonder that travellers heaved a sigh of relief when they had passed the heath in safety. Sometimes the thieves were caught, but not often, as the large shrubs in the forest hard by afforded ample cover to these evil-doers, and aided their escape.*

He added that 'Tradition, resting on some support, however, says that the notorious Dick Turpin was, at one period of his exciting career, a familiar figure on the heath'. Non-professional highwaymen also occasionally tried their luck. It is reported that in 1789 a carriage was held up there by a lone masked man, who took three guineas from the passengers then apologized to them, saying that he 'only needed three to pay a debt' and couldn't think of another way of getting the money.

According to early newspapers, many of these robberies took place at the junction of the High Road and Whalebone Lane. On 22 January 1787, for example, *The Times* reported that as a Mr Scott was returning to London one evening from Romford, he was stopped 'near the Whalebones' by 'two footpads, but being armed with a blunderbuss he fired on them, and shot one dead on the spot; the other made his escape'. Whalebones have been associated with this junction since at least 1641, and it appears that several sets have been placed there over the years.

Whalebone House, just east of the junction, had two huge bones overhanging its gates. Another pair was set up next to the toll-gate at which travellers had to pay a fee for using the turnpike road. Contemporary maps appear to show that the octagonal-shaped toll house was first situated on the north-western side of the junction (where the *Toll Gate* pub now stands), and later rebuilt on the south-western corner. The gate itself stretched between the toll house and the opposite side of the High Road. At right-angles to it was a bar crossing Whalebone Lane on the south side, so that travellers heading towards Beacontree Heath also had to pay.

Terror at the Toll Gate, 1829

In 1829 the keeper of the Whalebone tollgate was George Smith. He lived in the toll house, and his job came with the constant inconvenience of being awakened in the middle of the night. Towards the end of November he was roused not long after midnight by the sound of thumping on the door and a voice impatiently calling 'Gate!' Smith hauled himself out of his warm bed, threw on a coat, seized his bunch of keys and went down. 'All right, I'm coming', he shouted.

As he opened the door and stepped out, he was seized from behind and his eyes covered by a pair of hands. Smith cried 'Murder!' upon which the attackers threatened to shoot him. The terrified man begged to be released, saying he would make no resistance. One of the three assailants answered 'We will take bloody good care you do not'. They threw him to the ground, took off his cap, held it over his mouth to silence him, then rifled his pockets of about 25 shillings. One of the men then entered the house, seized a poker and broke open a cupboard and the till, but found only about £3 in cash, including three crown pieces and a battered sixpence.

Middlesex & Essex
Turnpike Roads.
WHALEBONE Gate.
This Ticket clears
Whitechapel, Mile End
Stratford
Romford
Whalebone
Woodford Bridge
Putwell Bridge
and all other Gates and
Bars on this Trust.
28

A toll ticket from the Whalebone turnpike gate LBBD Archives at Valence House Museum

Having secured the money, the thieves handed Smith back his cap. Cheekily wishing him 'Good night!' they rode off towards London. At this time the road was protected at night by the Bow Street Mounted Patrol, so Smith waited for the arrival of George Weston, the officer patrolling the Romford to Ilford section. It being a dark, wintry night, Smith had not been able to get a good look at his attackers. All he could say to Weston was that one was about 5 feet 6 inches tall, thin and active, and wore a black coat and dark trousers. The second was a tall man, and he saw nothing at all of the third.

Weston galloped off in pursuit. He was told the riders had passed through Ilford, but was unable to trace them beyond the turning to Wanstead Flats. Although he gave information to the Mile End turnpike gate within two hours of the robbery, the culprits melted away into the darkness. The crime had clearly been well-planned. Weston discovered that earlier that night three men had enquired at Ilford whether the Romford patrol had gone forward. They had pretended that they wanted to claim his protection on the road, but no doubt their real purpose was to ensure they avoided him. They knew he would be at the Romford end of the road while they were robbing George Smith at the Whalebone Gate.

The Poisoned Watchdog, 1845

Sixteen years later, criminals struck at Whalebone Cottage, situated on the north side of the High Road, just east of the Whalebone junction. This was a substantial, recently-built house with eight rooms, stable, carriage houses and other outbuildings. Its land included a kitchen-garden and a large paddock. The owner was Jonathan Arnold, a prosperous retired stockbroker in his sixties, who lived with his wife Mercy and their two servants. Knowing the dangers of the High Road, Mr Arnold had taken precautions against theft, keeping his valuables in a chest 'of prodigious strength and weight' screwed down inside a cupboard in the dining room. They also kept a watchdog.

On the evening of 19 November 1845, servant Emma Cornwell locked up the house at about 10 p.m., and soon afterwards the household went to bed. Just before 6 a.m. the following morning, Emma came downstairs only to discover the back hall door was wide open. Much alarmed, she immediately ran upstairs to inform Mr and Mrs Arnold. When Mr Arnold came down into the dining room, he was shocked to find a large hedge stake on the table. He looked towards the cupboard, and saw that his iron chest was missing. The burglars had evidently gained their entrance by first removing a panel from the back door.

As soon as daylight dawned, Mr Arnold went over to the paddock behind the house. He found the missing door panel on the ground, full of gimlet-holes. The iron chest lay nearby, broken open, and some of the documents it contained were strewn about. Among the items missing from the chest were £70 in Bank of England notes, £40 in gold sovereigns and a silver watch. A work table had been carried out of the house, and was found higher up the same field, the drawers taken out and broken. Mr Arnold had wondered why his watchdog had not barked at the robbers, but the sad explanation was now all too obvious. The dog was lying by the side of the chest, dead. It had been given food laced with prussic acid.

PC James Crawford was quickly on the scene, arriving at about 7 a.m. Looking closely at the ground, he saw two sets of footprints across the paddock. They also appeared in the adjoining ploughed field. Crawford followed the trail across several fields, down a lane and into a garden attached to a cottage. He knew that two men named Joseph Walker, 24, and his lodger William Walden, 28, both timber hewers, lived there. Crawford asked where they were, and was told that they had gone to Romford. He headed straight there and at about 11 a.m. spotted the pair and immediately arrested them. He took their shoes away, and found that they matched the prints on the ground. Walker had upon him a sovereign, two half-crowns and other silver, totalling 33 shillings. The police searched Walker's house and found a gimlet. It was rusty, but had apparently been recently used. Had it removed the panel of the back door of Whalebone Cottage?

The prisoners appeared before the Ilford magistrates the following Saturday, and were sent for trial at the next Essex Assizes. In March 1846 they accordingly appeared at the Shire Hall in Chelmsford. The prosecution offered no additional evidence, and Mr Marsh, the defence counsel, addressed the jury upon what he considered to be the 'extreme weakness' of the case against the prisoners. The presiding judge, Lord Denman, was beginning to sum up the evidence when the foreman of the jury interrupted. He said that they would spare His Lordship the trouble, as they all agreed that the prisoners were not guilty.

In the meantime, one of the stolen £5 Bank of England notes had been traced. A man named William Dunn used note number 24,564 to pay for a joint of meat from a butcher in Southwark. He was arrested on suspicion of involvement in the burglary, but it seems that the charge was subsequently dropped due to lack of evidence.

Frightened by the whole experience, Jonathan and Mercy Arnold decided to leave as soon as possible. *The Times* printed a notice of the auction of Whalebone Cottage at Garraway's at 2 p.m. on Tuesday, 13 January 1846. The elderly couple then settled in Harley Place, Bow. Jonathan died there in February 1857 aged 78, and Mercy followed in 1864. Their former home had evidently remained close to their hearts, however, as they chose to be buried at Dagenham parish church. In his

The memorial to Jonathan and Mercy Arnold inside Dagenham Parish Church. Authors' collection

A mid-twentieth century view of Whalebone Cottage when in use as a library. The original house can be seen in the centre of the picture. LBBD Archives at Valence House Museum

will, Jonathan bequeathed £100 in consols to establish a charity to maintain his tomb and help 'the deserving poor'. A plaque to the memory of the couple was placed on the wall inside the church.

Whalebone Cottage later became known as Elgin Lodge, and in the 1930s it was purchased by Dagenham Council. With extensions to the front and later to the rear, the building entered the final phase of its history as Whalebone Library. It was a landmark in the area until its demolition in 1999. The car park of the new Robert Jeyes Library marks the site of the old building.

Sources

Chelmsford Chronicle
The Times
The *Essex Standard*
Will of Jonathan Arnold (National Archives, PROB 11/2247)

Chapter 3

Murder or Suicide? The Strange Case of Mary Dunsdon 1845

They asked me whether I saw anyone splashed with blood, and I told them 'no-one only you'.

Just a month before the robbery at Whalebone Cottage, a death had taken place elsewhere in Chadwell Heath that would make national headlines and create a mystery which has endured to the present day.

If, back in October 1845, a traveller left Whalebone Cottage and proceeded westwards along the High Road for about a mile, he would arrive at the *Cooper's Arms* beer house. At this point a road named Wangey Lane went off to the left, leading towards the railway line and ancient Wangey House. A cluster of houses stood on the eastern side of the lane, one of which was occupied by the Dunsdon family. Thomas Francis

By the time of this early twentieth century photograph, Wangey Lane had been re-named Station Road. LBBD Archives at Valence House Museum

Dunsdon and his wife Mary Maria (formerly Howell), both 38, were originally from Barking, where they had married in February 1829. They had three sons and a daughter. Thomas Dunsdon had worked as an agricultural labourer before becoming a potato salesman for Francis Glenny of nearby Chadwell Heath Farm. He went to market three times a week and proved a reliable employee. While Thomas's prospects were rising, the health of his wife Mary was showing great cause for concern. By the autumn of 1845 she was largely bedridden due to a lumbar abscess arising from spinal disease.

The Dunsdons rented a house from linen draper George Banham, who lived next door with his wife Faith Louisa. Early in the morning of Monday, 20 October 1845 Mrs Banham crossed the yard between the two houses to visit the invalid, bringing her a breakfast of a boiled egg, bread and butter and cup of tea.

At about 8.45 a.m. a doctor named Robert Bowie, a Scotsman in his fifties, arrived to see Mrs Dunsdon. Bowie rented Valence House, a medieval moated manor in Dagenham less than a mile away. He described the pain Mrs Dunsdon was suffering as 'one of the most excruciating that can be endured'. That morning he found her 'very much depressed in spirits', telling him she thought she would never recover. The sympathetic medical man reassured her that 'I was in hope she would'. Another abscess, possibly a bedsore, had appeared on Mrs Dunsdon's leg. Bowie examined it and told her to 'Keep on with the poultice and it will do very well'. His visit lasted between five and ten minutes.

Thomas and Mary Dunsdon had one servant, Rachel Simmons, who had joined them only nine or ten days before. About half an hour after Bowie's departure, Rachel entered Mrs Dunsdon's room and asked if she should make the bed. She was told 'No, there's no need, Mrs Banham has made it straight'. Mrs Dunsdon then instructed Rachel to boil a piece of mutton and make some broth for dinner. Rachel went downstairs to fetch the meat from the larder and begin cooking. A few minutes later she saw Thomas Dunsdon enter the back parlour. He took off his hat and coat and hung them up behind the door. He poured himself a cup of coffee, but before drinking it said 'I am going upstairs'.

Rachel then left to do some work in the yard. Shortly afterwards, at about 9.45 a. m., she heard Thomas Dunsdon shrieking 'She has done it, she has done it!' Rachel dashed into the house and towards the staircase leading up to Mrs Dunsdon's bedroom. As she ran up she passed

Dunsdon coming down. On entering the room, Rachel saw Mrs Dunsdon lying flat upon her back in bed, both hands lying on her chest, blood pouring from her throat. Rachel immediately ran down again in search of help.

Meanwhile, their neighbour George Banham had burst into the house on hearing the shrieks and gone up into the bedroom. He shouted down to Rachel to bring some towels. Banham put his hand under Mrs Dunsdon's neck and raised her up onto his left arm. He held the towels to her throat and prayed aloud 'Lord have mercy, Lord have mercy'. Her husband came half way up the stairs and called out 'Is it fatal?' Banham told him to go back down, as 'She won't last another ten minutes'. Banham later memorably described the gash on Mrs Dunsdon's throat: 'You might have put a pint bottle end-ways into it.' She died six or seven minutes after he entered the room.

A surgeon, Charles Butler, was soon on the scene. He confirmed the size of the wound, reporting that it 'commenced from nearly underneath the right ear, carried very deeply down through the arteries and veins and through the windpipe quite down to the bones of the neck, going on the opposite side almost to underneath the left ear'. George Banham had noticed 'no blood about the bed when I went into the room, but blood was running both sides down her neck. When I entered the room the upper part of the bedclothes were perfectly smooth, no appearance of any struggle'.

Two days later, on 22 October, an inquest was held at the nearby *Cooper's Arms* before Charles Carne Lewis, coroner for south Essex. The verdict was that Mary Dunsdon had killed herself 'while labouring under temporary insanity'. Her body was released for burial at St Margaret's Church in Barking, where she had been baptized and married.

As they left the inquest, George Banham and Rachel Simmons were far from happy. The jury had insisted they only spoke about the scene in Mrs Dunsdon's room as she lay dying. When Banham tried to tell them of other things he had seen and heard that morning, he was cut short. That didn't stop him speaking his mind elsewhere, however. A day or two after the inquest Dunsdon gave Banham written notice that he was quitting his tenancy of the house. Banham reported that Dunsdon said he would 'serve me with *another* piece of paper', presumably meaning that he would take some legal action. And little wonder. What had reached Dunsdon's ears was the allegation that he had cut his own wife's throat. When local magistrate Octavius Mashiter heard the rumours he interviewed Banham and Rachel, and then summoned Dunsdon to appear before the Ilford magistrates at the *Angel Inn* on a charge of murder.

Dunsdon stood at the bar dressed in his work clothes, and reporters noticed that during part of the hearing he 'fondled one of his children in a most affectionate manner'. Rachel Simmons was the first to give evidence. She said that Mrs Dunsdon had given no signs of eccentricity and 'I never noticed anything to lead me to suppose she was of unsound mind'. She claimed Mrs Dunsdon was often well enough to leave her bed and do needlework. Rachel stated that Mr Dunsdon had never communicated any fears that his wife was suicidal, and had not instructed her to keep knives and other sharp instruments out of reach.

Rachel told the magistrates that on the Saturday afternoon previous to Mrs Dunsdon's death, Thomas had come in from work and asked her how his wife was. Rachel told him that she was not quite so sick that day, and he allegedly replied 'I should have been happy to hear she was no more when I came home'. Rachel then went on to say that the following day, Sunday, she heard the couple having a violent quarrel. Rachel's next statement must have caused a gasp among the audience in the packed courtroom. She said that when she had passed Dunsdon on the stairs he was holding an open razor dripping with blood.

George Banham then took the stand. He explained that he had known the deceased woman for six or seven years, and 'never saw anything to induce me to think that Mrs Dunsdon was of unsound mind'. He was asked whether he had spread a rumour that Dunsdon had 'a woman in London', and that his wife knew of the affair, but Banham firmly denied this. He said that as soon as Mrs Dunsdon had breathed her last, his first thought was to find the knife she must have used. He had searched in the bed, on it, under it, and throughout the room, but there was no sign of a blade of any kind.

Banham had then gone down into the yard. He saw Thomas Dunsdon standing with Josiah Dickins, a local carpenter, and asked 'Where is this instrument that the fatal deed was done with?' Neither said a word, so he repeated 'There is an instrument that this was done with, and no one shall leave until it is found'. According to Banham, Josiah Dickins then said, in a low tone, 'I have got it'. Banham said 'Got what?' and Dickins replied 'The razor'. 'How came you by that, as you have not been upstairs?' Dickins allegedly told him 'I took it from Dunsdon's hand'. He then checked himself, and said 'I don't know whether I picked it off the bricks or no'. Dunsdon, apparently, was close enough to have heard the conversation, but said nothing.

Dickins then left to fetch the police, but Banham followed him to the road and asked 'Where *is* this razor?' Dickins replied he had hidden it behind some dishes on a shelf in the back kitchen. Banham headed straight for the kitchen to search for the razor, joined by Rachel Simmons, who eventually found it. As she handed it to Banham, she noticed that 'There was a little blood upon the blade, very little indeed'. Banham walked back to Dunsdon, still standing in the yard, and said 'What a bad job'. Dunsdon allegedly replied 'I am in no way sorry she is dead; she never would have been no more use to me or my family, for the Devil is always after those sort of people'. PC James Crawford soon arrived, and Banham handed him the razor. Two days later, after the inquest, Crawford had given the razor to Dickins and asked him to put it away. Unfortunately, the Ilford magistrates could not now examine it for themselves. Josiah Dickins admitted he had got rid of it by throwing it into a large pond at nearby Wangey House.

Banham went on to tell the magistrates that he didn't speak to Dunsdon again until the day of the inquest at the *Cooper's Arms*. After appearing before the jury, he had entered the tap-room and found Dunsdon there. Banham had said 'They asked me whether I saw anyone splashed with blood, and I told them no-one only you'. Dunsdon replied 'Am I?' and Banham said 'Is it not blood on your waistcoat?' Dunsdon remarked that it must be red paint, but Banham turned him towards the window, picked off some of the substance, and, breaking it between his fingernails, said 'This is blood'. Dunsdon then wondered 'I can't think how I came by it', to which Banham replied 'Why, from your wife'.

Mrs Amelia Humphreys stated that she had waited in the death chamber until the arrival of the surgeon, and had taken care not to touch the body during that time. The magistrates asked whether there had been blood on Mrs Dunsdon's hands, and she replied that 'There was a little blood on both the hands as if it had streamed down from the wound. I only observed blood between her fingers, she had one ring on her left hand. I took off that ring. I did not perceive on taking off the ring any blood in the open part of the hand, only blood between her fingers'. Mrs Humphreys went on to say that she and Mrs

Mary Dickins had looked after the house until after the funeral, and never saw any blood on Dunsdon or his clothes. She asserted that Dunsdon had been 'very low and melancholy on the morning of his wife's death'.

Josiah Dickins was called to give his evidence, and much of what he said contradicted George Banham's version of events. Dickins said he had rushed into the house, glanced into Mrs Dunsdon's bedroom, saw he was not needed and then went down into the back yard. He noticed a razor lying on the ground. About ten minutes later, Thomas Dunsdon had entered the yard, picked up the razor and said 'Where could she get this from?' Dickins stated he had then taken the razor from Dunsdon's hand and carried it into the kitchen. Dickins said he remembered Banham saying to Dunsdon it was a 'bad job', but claimed that Dunsdon's reaction had been 'Oh, that I had seen the last of her! Oh, that she had died a natural death!' Dickins firmly denied that Dunsdon had said he wasn't sorry his wife was dead, or that 'the Devil is always after these people'. Dickins declared he had seen no blood on Dunsdon's clothes, and that the bereaved man had 'shed tears and mourned. I stopped two hours with him to comfort him'.

Dunsdon's employer, Francis Glenny, a nonconformist minister who had recently built a new chapel nearby, also spoke up in his defence. He said that five days before the death Dunsdon had told him his wife's mind was in 'a very sad state'. That evening Glenny had called to see her and pray with her, and found 'her eyes rolling in their sockets'. The following day Dunsdon told Glenny that Mary had just attempted suicide. She had asked him to go down and boil the kettle, and on returning to the bedroom, he found the pillow had been moved slightly. Apparently Mary had then pulled out a knife from under the pillow, and handed it to him, saying 'Here it is, take it, for it will not do it'.

Robert Bowie, the surgeon who had seen Mrs Dunsdon an hour before her death, was also called. He stated that he 'was not at all surprised' that she should have committed suicide. He 'never saw anything but kindness from Dunsdon to his wife, and he was anxious I should do all I could for her'. Charles Butler, who had examined the body shortly after death, told the magistrates that the medical evidence was inconclusive on the question of whether or not the throat wound was self-inflicted. 'The deceased *might* have done it herself by either hand, such is my opinion...Such a wound *might* have been given by some other person'.

The magistrates sent Dunsdon for trial at the next Essex Assizes at

Chelmsford. Remarkably, for such a serious charge, they agreed to accept bail provided that Dunsdon pledged £500 himself plus two sureties of £500 each. Accordingly, in March 1846, the members of the Grand Jury gathered to hear the prosecution evidence before deciding whether the case should proceed to a full trial. After hearing the depositions, the Grand Jury debated the case in private, then announced that they were rejecting the indictment. Dunsdon was now a free man.

On 24 October 1846, twelve months after his wife's death, Thomas Dunsdon remarried. His new bride was Mary Ann Jones from Walworth in Surrey, and the ceremony took place at the Baptist Chapel in Mare Street, Hackney. The couple continued to live in Chadwell Heath, and Dunsdon eventually set himself up as a farmer on his own account. By the time of the 1861 census he was farming sixteen acres and employing five people. The scandal surrounding his first wife's death had clearly not hindered his career.

This intriguing case raises many questions. In Thomas Dunsdon's defence, it could be argued that on entering the room and finding that Mary had cut her throat, the shock and trauma of the moment may have caused him to grab the razor and wander downstairs with it, not knowing what he was doing. Josiah Dickins then perhaps put the razor in the kitchen, and later in the pond, to save his friend from having to look at it. Francis Glenny, an influential local figure, was, as we have seen, convinced of Dunsdon's innocence, and his defence barrister was not given the opportunity of presenting his version of events. Yet in the face of such a scandal it is surprising that Dunsdon, if innocent, did not make a public statement, perhaps in the form of a letter to a local newspaper. Instead, he remained absolutely silent, and as far as we know didn't carry out his threat to sue George Banham.

Mary Dunsdon was clearly in extreme pain, and had told Robert Bowie that same morning that she feared she would never recover. She seems an obvious candidate for suicide, yet statistics show that throat-cutting is usually done by men. A weak, ill woman would be more likely to take poison or an overdose of a drug such as laudanum. Another argument against her cutting her own throat is that both George Banham and Amelia Humphreys state that blood was running down her neck but was not on her hands or the bedclothes. If she had wielded the razor herself, cutting from ear to ear right down to the bones in her neck as reported by the surgeon, blood would surely have spurted out over the hand holding the blade.

The appearance of the scene – the bedclothes smooth and undisturbed, the hands lying on her chest – may even suggest that Mary Dunsdon, far from carrying out the act herself, had been asleep when it was done. We may even consider whether it had been an assisted suicide. Did she perhaps beg her husband to carry out what she was not strong enough to do herself?

Thomas Dunsdon died at East Street in his home town of Barking on 8 January 1866. He was 58 years old and had suffered a heart attack. He alone knew the truth of what happened on 20 October 1845, and took it with him to the grave.

Sources

Depositions (National Archives, ASSI 36/5)
The *Essex Standard*
The *Chelmsford Chronicle*

Chapter 4

Cornfield Killing: the Murder of PC George Clark 1846

Clark was lying on his back with his legs crossed, a sheaf of corn clutched tightly in his right hand.

On the evening of Sunday, 28 June 1846, the congregation of the Methodist Chapel in Bull Street, Dagenham, awaited the preacher. When he did not arrive, a young man volunteered to take the service. He was 20 year old George Clark, and wore his police officer's uniform of tailcoat and white trousers. Clark had only been in Dagenham for six weeks. He had already demonstrated his commitment to the Methodist cause by distributing tracts as he went round his beat. At the close of the service, he told his audience 'Perhaps we may not all meet again in this world, but if not God be with you'. This proved to be a prophetic statement. The very next day, George Clark was brutally murdered.

Bull Street, Dagenham Village. The little girls in the middle distance to the left of the picture are standing against the weatherboarded police station where Clark lived and served. LBBD Archives at Valence House Museum

Clark had been born in Battlesden, Bedfordshire, into a family of agricultural labourers. On his nineteenth birthday, 2 June 1845, he enrolled in London's Metropolitan Police. He was assigned to K Division, and his first posting was at Arbour Square, Stepney, close to the notorious Ratcliffe Highway. Clark lived and worked for almost a year at Arbour Square, then on 15 May 1846 he and his colleague Isaac Hickton were transferred to the sleepy village of Dagenham. They were needed there because three Dagenham officers had recently been thrown out of the force after beating up an ostler at the *Cross Keys*, flourishing their cutlasses at anyone daring to intervene.

Clark's new home, Dagenham Police Station, was very different from the modern purpose-built accommodation at Arbour Square. It was a cottage on the western side of Bull Street, described as a 'very old brick wood and lathe and plaster house with stable for one horse and weather board lockup'. When the K Division had been extended to Dagenham in January 1840, their welcome was not exactly warm. The *Chelmsford Chronicle* reported that PC Thomas Norton was attacked by a mob in Dagenham Village chanting 'No Police! No Police!'

This early photograph of the Chase approach at Eastbrookend conveys a sense of the lonely country roads on Clark's beat. LBBD Archives at Valence House Museum

George Clark was given the Eastbrookend beat, which began at the Four Wants junction and included some very lonely country lanes. He patrolled alone and on foot between 9 p.m. and 6 a.m., carrying a rattle to raise the alarm and a cutlass and truncheon with which to defend himself. On Monday, 29 June 1846 Clark went on duty as usual, walking to the beginning of his beat with his sergeant William Parsons. He was seen by farm labourer Luke White at about 10.30 p.m., striding along singing a hymn.

When Clark failed to return to the station at the end of his shift, his colleagues began searching the area around his beat, concentrating on dragging the many ponds in case he had lost his way in the darkness and drowned. Four days later, on the evening of 3 July, a search party arrived at Thorntons Farm, Rush Green. The farmer's wife, Elizabeth Page, told them about a pond at the edge of a cornfield belonging to neighbouring farmer William Parfey Collier. As they approached the pond they became aware of a foul smell, and PC Thomas Kimpton spotted a truncheon lying in a ditch, covered with blood and hair. Mrs Page's 12 year old son William ran ahead. He saw a police cutlass sticking out of a hedge, then spun round and almost stumbled on Clark's body.

Clark was lying on his back with his legs crossed, a sheaf of corn clutched tightly in his right hand. There was a gaping wound across his throat, so deep that it cut through his leather choker and windpipe. Clark also had a stab wound in the back of his neck which severed his spinal cord, and another under his left ear which nearly came out on the other side. Clark's body and face were very bruised, and he lay in a pool of blood in which were found pieces of his skull. The forefinger of his left hand was almost cut through. His money, rattle and silver watch were still in his pockets. The watch had stopped at 3 o'clock. The spot was a quarter of a mile from Clark's beat.

Clark's body was taken on a cart to Hunters Hall Farm, where a Romford surgeon, Joseph Collin, carried out a post-mortem. The following day, 4 July, the inquest opened, presided over by Coroner Charles Carne Lewis. Sergeant William Parsons stated that he had met Clark as usual at 1 a.m., but that he hadn't turned up for their next planned meeting two hours later. Abia Butfoy, Clark's predecessor on the Eastbrookend beat, told the Coroner that he had been threatened by a Romford man named William Walker. This encounter had caused Butfoy to be taken off the beat and replaced by George Clark, and he believed that Clark had been killed in mistake for himself. The inquest was adjourned so that Scotland Yard detectives could make further enquiries. Clark's mother, Charlotte insisted on viewing her son's body, although the Coroner advised against it. She collapsed and had to be helped away.

George Clark was buried in Dagenham Parish Churchyard the following day, Sunday, 5 July. He had been engaged to Elizabeth How, who lived near his home village in Bedfordshire, and it is believed that the couple were to have been married that very day. Posters offering a £100 reward for information leading to the conviction of his killers were widely distributed. The inquest reopened at the *Cross Keys* in Dagenham Village on 11 July. William Walker's brother Amos spoke up vehemently, defending him against Butfoy's accusations. A new twist was provided by the evidence of Mrs Elizabeth Page of Thorntons Farm. She claimed that PC Thomas Kimpton had told her that Sergeant Parsons, far from meeting Clark at 1 a.m. as he had claimed under oath at the first hearing, had in fact not been on duty that night. Kimpton and Parsons both denied this, and were backed up by constables Isaac Hickton, John Farnes, Jonas Stevens and Abia Butfoy. The argument continued at the third inquest hearing twelve days later, and there was uproar as Parsons lost his temper, shouting that they were 'endeavouring to prove him the murderer'.

On 15 August 1846 the Police Commissioners at Scotland Yard were visited by Abia Butfoy, who confessed that the Dagenham officers had indeed lied on the subject of Parsons being on duty. He claimed that on 29 June he and the sergeant had been drinking all day in various Romford and Dagenham pubs. By late afternoon Butfoy was very drunk, so Parsons apparently excused him from going on duty that night. Parsons himself had then gone to bed at midnight, asking Kimpton to take the horse and do duty for him. All the Dagenham officers, including Butfoy, were promptly suspended from duty and put under house arrest. When the inquest resumed on 20 August, Butfoy's fellow constables all confessed that Parsons had told them to say he had been on duty the night of the murder. Parsons, however, continued to deny it.

The final inquest hearing took place on 22 September. In his summing up, the Coroner stated that Clark's extensive injuries showed that his murder was a revenge attack. He spoke about the movements of Clark's colleagues on the fatal night, concentrating on Parsons and Butfoy. Could they *prove* they were elsewhere at the time? The jury eventually returned a verdict of 'Wilful murder against some person or persons unknown'.

National newspapers had followed every twist and turn of the sensational case. Some, including *The Times*, were shocked at the evidence of a culture of dishonesty and drunkenness within the police force. Editorials called for a public enquiry which could have threatened the continued existence of the Metropolitan Police. Anxious to restore public confidence, the police authorities wanted to prosecute the officers. Eventually, charges were brought against three – Parsons for conspiracy and Kimpton and Hickton for perjury. In February, however, the trio managed to slip away from Dagenham. Kimpton soon gave himself up, but a poster offering a £50 reward was circulated with descriptions of Parsons and Hickton.

In June 1847 Isaac Hickton, in hiding in Liverpool, saw the poster and decided to give himself up. He wrote to his father, asking him to tell an old school friend, Sergeant George Hardy of the Derby Police, to come and arrest him. He hoped that his father and Hardy would share the reward. The following month, Hickton and Thomas Kimpton were tried for perjury at the Essex Assizes at the Shire Hall, Chelmsford. They were found guilty, and sentenced to be fined one shilling, imprisoned for one week, then transported for seven years. In September 1847 they were sent to Millbank Prison. On Christmas Eve of that year, Kimpton was transferred to the convict hulks moored off Woolwich. In January 1848 Hickton was sent to Northampton Gaol. His mental state was giving cause for concern, which may be the reason he did not go to the hulks with Kimpton.

William Parsons, meanwhile, had remained at large until July 1847. He found work on the construction of the Lincoln to Grimsby railway line. Two policemen disguised as labourers tracked him down to the *Steam Packet* beer house in Lincoln. On 7 March 1848 he appeared in the dock at Chelmsford accused of conspiracy. The presiding judge, Lord Denman, surprised everyone present by stopping the trial, ruling that there was not enough evidence to support the charge. Parsons, now a free man, decided to emigrate to British Columbia with the Hudson's Bay Company on a five-year contract, managing a watermill. At the end of this time he purchased some nearby land by a bridge and built a public house and hotel there. It proved to be a great success. The disgraced sergeant had now made a new life for himself, and the area is called Parson's Bridge to this day.

Isaac Hickton and Thomas Kimpton were not transported, and were released in 1849. Their colleague Abia Butfoy died in distressing circumstances in Colney Hatch Lunatic Asylum aged only 43. His mind was consumed by the terrible events of George Clark's death. A doctor reported that towards the end of his life he was 'frequently restless – shouting in his sleep crying "Murder, Murder" '.

By 1858, twelve years after the killing of Clark, no one had yet been charged with his murder. Then, on 24 June of that year, Inspector Jonathan Whicher, the most celebrated detective of his day, strode into Farmer Seabrook's field in Dagenham. He approached George Blewitt, an elderly farm labourer, and announced he was arresting him on suspicion of the murder of Clark.

This sensational turn of events had been prompted by new evidence from a Mrs Mary Ann Smith. In 1846 she had been the wife of a farm worker named William Page, and lived in a cottage on Clark's beat. Her original depositions, full of vivid and forceful language, survive in the National Archives. She claimed that on the evening of 29 June 1846 she had pleaded with Clark to persuade her husband, who was violent towards her, to mend his ways. Clark had accordingly stopped Page and given him a lecture about his immortal soul, but this only had the effect of enraging him. Page came home in a foul mood and announced to his wife that he and three other men, Ned Wood, George Chalk and George Blewitt, planned to stage a robbery that night, and that if Clark interfered they would 'stab the b___ down to the ground'.

Mrs Smith alleged that just after midnight the four men, taking her as lookout, entered the barn at Eastbrookend Old Hall, belonging to farmer Thomas Waters Brittain. They intended to steal sacks of corn and take them to neighbouring farmer, Ralph Page, who would be waiting in his barn at Thorntons Farm. Clark had come upon them, was beaten unconscious and taken to the cornfield where he was brutally killed.

Most of the suspects named by Mrs Smith were dead by 1858. Ned Wood had hanged himself, William Page had fallen beneath the wheels of his own cart, and Ralph Page was suspected of committing suicide by taking an overdose of laudanum. George Chalk, only 16 at the time of the murder, had emigrated to Australia. The only one still in the area was George Blewitt, who had been Mr Brittain's horse keeper at the time of the murder and had keys to the barn. The Grand Jury heard the evidence against him at the Essex Assizes, but the case was thrown out because Mrs Smith's evidence was not corroborated. Blewitt's defence suggested that Mrs Smith was 'of unsound mind' – she claimed to have seen the ghost of her husband, as well as the Devil and even the apparition of a fire-engine in her bedroom. She was elderly, deaf, poorly educated and presented as an object of ridicule.

No other arrests were made in the Clark case, yet it has provoked much discussion and many theories over the years. Could it have been mistaken identity? Was Clark murdered by enemies from his time at Arbour Square? He was said to be popular with young ladies, including the wife of Sergeant Parsons. Was he perhaps killed by a jealous husband? Clark was certainly a religious young man. Did his colleagues decide to shut him up in case he reported them for corruption? Did he perhaps discover that they were in league with smugglers, who plied their trade along this section of the Thames? Or was Mrs Smith right all along about the corn-stealers?

The restored memorial to George Clark in Dagenham Parish Churchyard. Lee Shelden

Clark has never been forgotten by the people of Dagenham. In 1996 a series of events took place to mark the 150th anniversary of his murder. His memorial in Dagenham Parish Churchyard was restored, and a tree was planted to his memory in Eastbrookend Country Park, close to his beat. The roads that Clark knew around Eastbrookend have not greatly changed since his day, and local legend has it that Clark still strides along the lonely road from the Four Wants.

Sources

Murder file (National Archives, MEPO 3/53)
Depositions (National Archives, ASSI 36/9)
Rhodes, Linda, Shelden, Lee & Abnett, Kathryn: *The Dagenham murder: the brutal killing of PC George Clark, 1846* (2005)

Chapter 5

The City Gent and the Tramp: Thomas Toller 1853

...with the bloody knife in one hand and heavy stick in the other, replied 'Well, he tried to murder me, and now I have murdered him'.

Six years after the death of George Clark, another horrifying local murder case filled the national newspaper columns. The tragic chain of events began in December 1852 as 47 year old Thomas Samuel Toller, a stockbroking commission agent, strolled along the Mile End Road at the end of his day's work. Toller was hailed by his friend and neighbour, Thomas Smith, who stopped and offered him a lift home to Chadwell Heath in his horse and trap. While Toller was getting in, they were approached by a tramp, a 'most forbidding, morose-looking man' in his early thirties. The tramp, whose name was Charles Saunders, asked for a few pence to help with that night's lodging. Smith refused to give him anything, demanding 'Why don't you work for a living? You are as well able to work as myself'. Thomas Toller weighed in with 'I've seen him around before, he's a regular impostor'. He said that if a police constable happened to come by, he would have Saunders arrested. Smith tried to calm things down by advising Saunders to 'toddle off' about his business. Toller repeated 'We have nothing to give you', and Saunders replied ominously 'I should like to give *you* something'.

Two months later, on Tuesday, 8 February 1853, Toller left home at 8 a.m. to walk along the Chadwell Heath High Road to Ilford Station in order to catch the London train. His neighbours described him as a 'very respectable and worthy man, very quiet, peaceable and inoffensive'. Toller was from a privileged background, being the son of the late Sir Samuel Toller, Advocate General of Madras and author of the standard textbooks

Toller's Law of Executors and *Toller on Tithes*. Yet Thomas Toller's financial circumstances had declined in recent years, and he was now barely scraping a living, earning only commission and not regular wages. He had married Ellen Blackmore in December 1840 and they had three sons and a daughter, with another baby on the way.

That morning, as we have seen, Toller set off on foot towards Ilford. After about a mile he reached the junction with Barley Lane. A figure was leaning against the hand post. It was the tramp, Charles Saunders, and he was holding a heavy bludgeon. A man named Thomas Willis was at work in a garden near the roadside. He became aware of raised voices coming from the direction of the crossroads, followed by a cry for help. Willis looked up to see Saunders knock off Toller's hat. Toller picked it up and began running back the way he had come, but Saunders followed, caught him up and then began raining blows upon his head with the bludgeon. Toller fell to the ground, calling out 'Murder! Murder!' and holding up his hands in an attempt to defend himself.

Willis shouted to Saunders 'Leave off!' then jumped over the fence from the garden into the road and ran towards them. Another eyewitness, William Clark, also raced towards the scene. Before they could come to the aid of Toller, however, Saunders took a clasp knife from his pocket, five or six inches long. He opened it, stooped down, and plunged it into the side of Toller's neck. His victim ceased to struggle, and died almost immediately. Thomas Willis cried 'Why, you have killed the man!' Saunders, with the bloody knife in one hand and heavy stick in the other, replied 'Well, he tried to murder me, and now I have murdered him'. He then ran off up Barley Lane towards Hainault Forest. The time was about 8.45 a.m.

Willis quickly alerted the police, who moved Toller's body to the nearby *Greyhound* pub and ordered an immediate manhunt. Meanwhile, Saunders had buried his knife and thrown the stick away in a stubble field. About half an hour later he passed through Aldborough Hatch Gate and into the forest. He was now around a mile and a half from the murder scene. Saunders was not familiar with the area, however, and quickly lost his bearings. Intending to go westwards towards London, he wandered in the opposite direction and found himself at the *Thatched House* beer shop at Little Heath, where he stopped to buy a half-pennyworth of tobacco and some lucifer matches.

It so happened that John Gaywood, a butcher of Chadwell Heath, had also stopped at the beer shop with his horse and cart to make a delivery.

The High Road, with the site of Toller's murder in the distance. The Greyhound *pub, on the left, was the venue for the inquest.* LBBD Archives at Valence House Museum

He knew Toller well, and had been shocked to hear of the murder. Saunders asked the road to London and then left. Gaywood noticed that his two greyhounds followed the tramp, which rather surprised him, as they were normally shy creatures. He resolved to follow Saunders, and tracked him southwards down Barley Lane. Being ignorant of the area, Saunders didn't realize that he was in fact walking back towards the murder scene.

At about 10.15 a.m. PC John Wilson Metcalf was standing at the junction of Barley Lane and the High Road. He caught sight of Saunders, 'a rough-looking fellow', walking towards him with blood on his trousers. Metcalf questioned him, and the man replied that he had cut his finger with a flint stone. He unwrapped a piece of rag from his finger and showed a still-bleeding wound. It seemed an innocent explanation, and Metcalf hesitated to take the man into custody, but John Gaywood then drove up and voiced his suspicions. Thomas Willis, the eyewitness, had returned to work in the nearby garden, but he was called over and immediately identified Saunders as the killer.

Metcalf then handcuffed Saunders and put him into Gaywood's cart. The vital witness Willis was ordered to get in too, and the four of them set off towards Ilford Police Station. As they ambled along in the butcher's cart, among the haunches of meat and strings of sausages, Saunders admitted his guilt. He announced 'I will tell you the truth; he once attempted to murder me, and now I have murdered him. He once hindered me from getting fourpence and a night's lodging, and something to eat, and there are four or five others that I would serve the same if I had time and opportunity'.

Saunders had only been in the police station a few hours when Superintendent Daniel Howie prepared to remove him to Ilford Gaol. A large and angry crowd had gathered outside, and the press reported that 'If it had not been for the presence of a large body of police and the exhortations of Mr Howie, the mob would have torn him to pieces'. Saunders was thrust into a light chaise-cart, the Superintendent whipped up the horses, and the crowd was forced to scatter as the vehicle sped off. The people had to be content with visiting the murder scene which, we are told, 'was too well indicated by the blood of the unfortunate man on the ground'. Coincidentally this spot, which was close to a short road called Stoup (or Stoop) Lane, had achieved infamy sixty years before. On 8 December 1794, a King's Messenger named James Martin was shot and killed there by five highwaymen, who were never captured.

With great rapidity, the south Essex coroner, Charles Carne Lewis, opened the inquest into Toller's death at the *Greyhound* pub that same afternoon. A surgeon, Edward Sullivan, announced that he had carried out a post-mortem: 'I examined him and found contused wounds on the head; three fingers on the right hand were broken; there were two gashes – one about the chin, and one extending through the windpipe and reaching down to the spine.' On 22 February Saunders was moved from Ilford Gaol to Newgate to await trial at the Old Bailey. As he was being taken by road through Stratford, hundreds of sightseers clamoured for a glimpse of him.

Some newspapers had claimed that Toller was in the habit of carrying large sums of money to and from London, but this was denied. The *Essex Standard* pointed out that, on the contrary, Toller's family had been left in a 'destitute condition' and 'utterly unprovided for'. It appeared that the eldest boy, aged 12, was deaf and dumb and had now been sent to an institution at Brighton. The banking houses of Coutts and

Masterman & Co. launched appeals to raise money for Toller's widow and children.

On Thursday, 3 March 1853 the trial of Charles Saunders began. His defence counsel, Mr Sleigh, did not dispute the facts of the case, but appealed to the jury to find Saunders not guilty by reason of insanity. We have already seen that while being taken to Ilford Police Station Saunders claimed, unbelievably, that Toller had tried to murder *him*. Charlotte Collyer, 33, a sister of Saunders, told the court that he had wandered about the country for the past fifteen years or so. She had frequently asked him why he tramped and did not work, but he didn't seem to understand what she was saying. About a month before the attack on Toller her brother had called at her house in an anxious state, babbling about the Roman Catholic religion and claiming that men were following him wherever he went with intention of killing him. Before entering her home he had looked about in all directions and examined the doors. Caroline stated that their mother had died in a lunatic asylum.

After hearing the evidence, the jury retired for twenty minutes before announcing a guilty verdict. When asked if he had anything to say before the death sentence was passed, Saunders said 'I am innocent; I only did it in my own defence'. The judge then pronounced: 'You will be taken to the place from whence you came, and from thence to the place of execution, and that you there be hanged by the neck until you are dead, and that your body be afterwards buried within the precincts of the gaol in which you shall be last confined after your conviction; and may the Lord have mercy on your soul.'

Many observers of the trial joined relatives of Saunders in appealing against the sentence. On 18 March a deputation travelled to Whitehall to present a petition to the Home Secretary, Lord Palmerston. Signed by the High Sheriff of Essex and many others, it claimed that Saunders was unable to distinguish right from wrong. Palmerston noted, however, that 'I have expressed to the deputation who gave me today this petition my regret that I do not feel it consistent with my duty to interfere in any way between the sentence of the law and its execution in this case'.

The defence counsel Mr Sleigh forwarded other letters of support. Mr Nash, a nurseryman of Mortlake in Surrey, wrote that he had known Saunders nearly all his life, and he 'appeared very strange and as if he was not right in his intellect'. Saunders had apparently worked for him on several occasions about seven years before, but kept leaving suddenly. 'When I remonstrated, he said he could not help it, turned his head away whilst he was talking and after I left him he would laugh. I have often heard people say "Here comes silly Charley Saunders".' A policeman wrote that Saunders told him: 'In the lodging house where I slept, I overheard them offer a man £2 to murder me.' According to a prison officer, Saunders had told him 'he would have killed two costermongers sometime since with his knife for striking him with a piece of mat. He would have killed a policeman at Woolwich Common for attempting to search him if he had proceeded'.

Caroline Collyer, Saunders's sister, recounted that 'he left Southampton last October because he imagined that the people of the place would kill him on account of so much rain having fallen'. He was said to have even tried to murder his own brother, Frederick. It was stated that about five years previously Saunders worked as a cook on board the barque *Caroline* to Sierra Leone and Guinea, but that during the voyage he had jumped overboard in a suicide attempt and was eventually hauled back up on a boat hook.

The hanging was due to take place above the entrance block of Springfield Gaol in Chelmsford on Wednesday, 23 March. Lord Palmerston decided to postpone it for a week pending medical reports, but the news only reached Chelmsford the day the execution was scheduled. Hundreds of people had already gathered on Springfield Hill. The *Essex Standard* noted disapprovingly that: 'We heard of one woman who (with a child in her arms), on being informed that the execution was deferred, avowed with evident disappointment that she had risen at four o'clock and walked from Billericay, a distance of ten miles, on purpose to be present.'

When the medical reports reached Lord Palmerston they did not succeed in changing his opinion. On 25 March he wrote that 'I cannot interfere. If I were to do so I should commit an offence against society.' So at 9 a.m. on 30 March 1853, preceded by the prison chaplain reading from the burial service, Charles Saunders was escorted from his cell. He shook hands with officials, exclaiming 'God bless you all', and was then handed over to the executioner. This was William Calcraft, the longest-serving hangman in history, described as 'a short, thickset shabby man' with 'venerable white locks, beard and sinister face'.

Press reporters noted that 'During the operation of pinioning, for a few seconds Saunders evinced a violent emotion, and trembled excessively,

A hanging above the gatehouse at Springfield Gaol, Chelmsford. Essex Record Office

but soon regained his indifference'. He climbed up the scaffold steps in front of about 300 to 400 spectators without assistance. As Calcraft placed a hood over his head and the rope around his neck, Saunders again cried out 'God bless you all!' The bolt was drawn almost immediately. According to the *Essex Standard*, 'He struggled in suspension for about half a minute, being rather a light weight, but upon the whole did not evince much suffering'. In this he was fortunate, as Calcraft favoured a short drop, meaning that his victims often endured slow strangulation.

On 22 August 1853, six and a half months after the murder, Thomas Toller's widow Ellen gave birth to a daughter, Agnes, at St Paul's Place in Islington. By the time of the 1871 census she and Agnes, now a 17 year old governess, were living at Moore's Cottages in Great Ilford. Ellen died aged 57 in November 1876 in Stoke Newington. By 1901 Agnes was working as a baker's assistant in Croydon. In a vivid illustration of the drastic social mobility that often occurred in Victorian England, it is doubtful whether customers would have believed that the woman behind the counter of the bakery was a grandchild of the eminent lawyer Sir Samuel Toller.

Sources

The Times
The *Essex Standard*
Petition and related correspondence (National Archives, HO 18/354)
Depositions, indictment and inquest (National Archives, CRIM 4/470)
Toller family genealogy at: http://www.gellibrand.com/surnames.html

Chapter 6

Lost at Sea

...one little boy was found in the cabin, the only one left to tell the tale of shipwreck and death...

A family tragedy, 1845

Visitors to St Margaret's Church in Barking will find many memorials that reflect the town's history as an important fishing port. Most poignant are the graves of those who lost their lives by drowning. A stone in the churchyard to the memory of the Byford family tells a particularly tragic story, one which took place not in a distant ocean but on the nearby River Thames.

At Barking Town Quay late in the evening of Wednesday, 5 February 1845, a sailing vessel known as a hatch-boat was being loaded with boxes of fish destined for Billingsgate Market. The boat's owner, William Byford, was a Lambeth-born lighterman and barge-owner who had moved to Barking in the mid-1830s. This had been a shrewd decision, for demand was high for the transport of cargo from Barking Creek to the London markets, and until 1854 there was no competition from the railway.

A Mr Day, a fisherman, had hired the vessel on this occasion, and a waterman named James Leach was employed to take charge of it during the voyage. Leach also hailed from Lambeth, so was probably a business associate of William Byford. Three passengers, wrapped up warm against the chilly winter night, also waited for the boat to depart. They were Edward, aged 20, William, 17, and Thomas, 13, the eldest children of William Byford and his wife Eliza. It is not recorded why the young men decided to take the trip. Were they on hand to help load and unload the cargo? Or did they intend to spend the day sightseeing in London? The three lads took their places and James Leach steered the boat down Barking Creek until it reached the Thames, then turned upriver towards the capital.

At between 1 a.m. and 2 a.m. the vessel was nearly opposite the *Devil's House*, a riverside inn about half way between Barking and Woolwich. The boat, with all sails set, was suddenly struck by a powerful gust of wind from the direction of west-north-west, and capsized almost immediately. Water rushed down the hatchway, trapping 13 year old Thomas Byford in the cabin. His brothers, together with Leach and Day, were flung into the water. They clung to the side of the upturned boat and called out for help, but unfortunately there were no other craft nearby. Soon afterwards the boat sank altogether, leaving them in the cold river, without lifejackets and weighed down by heavy winter clothing.

One by one, William and Edward Byford and Mr Day disappeared beneath the water. The waterman, James Leach, had been on the bowsprit (a pole projecting from the prow) when the boat capsized. Guessing that it would sink, he had immediately thrown off his jacket, which helped him stay afloat. After swimming for about twenty minutes, Leach was on the point of exhaustion when a man sailing past on a sand-brig heard his cries for help and pulled him aboard.

William and Eliza Byford, meanwhile, were asleep at their home in North Street, Barking. As well as the three boys on the boat, they had a younger son, John, and an 8 year old daughter Eliza. We do not know who broke the news, but apparently it was 'abruptly communicated' to the mother, 'leaving her nearly distracted'. Her husband was said to have borne his devastating loss 'with great fortitude'. Widespread sympathy was felt for them in the community, their sons being 'well known and esteemed for their good conduct and excellent characters'. There was sorrow too on

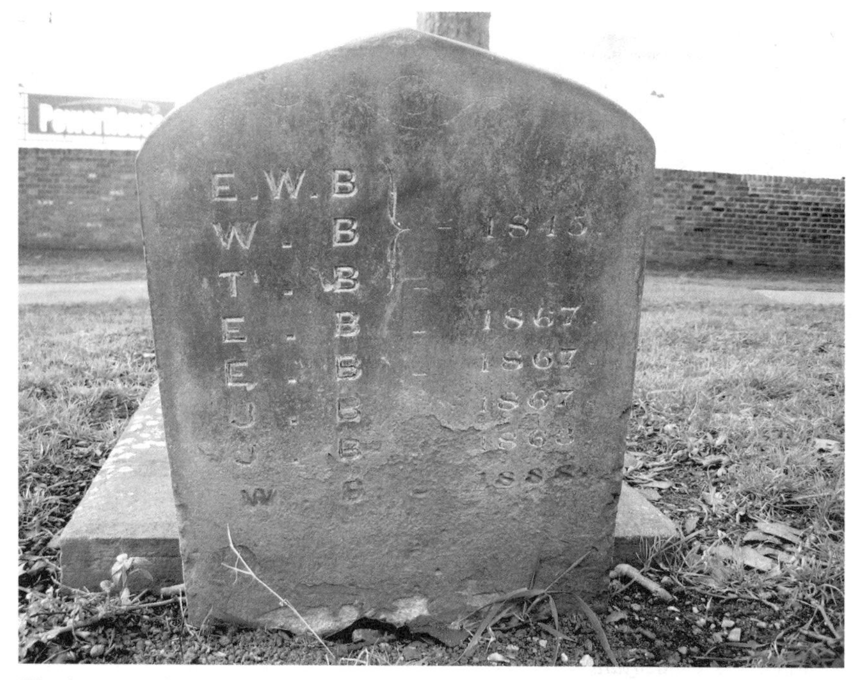

The footstone of the Byford grave, showing the initials of the three brothers drowned in 1845. Authors' collection

St Margaret's Churchyard. The Byford family grave can be seen in the foreground.
Authors' collection

behalf of Mrs Day, widow of the drowned fisherman, who had a young child and was expecting another.

It was rumoured that the vessel had been mown down in a collision with a steamer. This was disproved, however, by the evidence of James Leach, the sole survivor, and by the fact that when the boat was raised from the water a few days later it was found to be undamaged. The body of 13 year old Thomas Byford was discovered in the cabin, and on Monday, 10 February an inquest was held at the *George Inn*. The jury returned a verdict of accidental death, and Thomas was laid to rest in St Margaret's churchyard. Two months later the body of his brother Edward was buried alongside him, having been washed up near Woolwich. There is no record of the third brother, William, in the St Margaret's burial registers. Was his body swept out to sea, or eventually discovered too badly decomposed to be identified?

By the time of the 1851 census William Byford had expanded his business interests by taking over the *Jolly Waterman* beer house. He later went to live with his daughter Eliza and her husband Jesse Bailey at the *Peto Arms*, near Barking Station. When William Byford died in 1888 he was described in the *Essex Times* as an 'old and much respected inhabitant' of Barking. He had outlived his wife and all his children except his youngest son, John. William was buried in St Margaret's Churchyard on what would have been his 88th birthday. He lay at last alongside the sons he had mourned for over forty years.

The Great Storm, 1863

As we have seen, many Barking men and boys worked as fishermen. The occupation was a dangerous one, and there are numerous accounts of sinkings and fatalities. The night of Thursday, 3 December 1863 brought the heaviest toll. England was hit by the worst storm for many years, causing extensive damage and loss of life throughout the country, particularly on the eastern side.

When the storm burst, most of the Barking fishing fleet were off the coast of Holland, and were hit by a strong westerly wind which rapidly developed into a gale. The force of the waves completely overwhelmed some ships, and they sank with all their occupants. Some crews, for example those of the *Volante*, owned by Mr Morgan, were fortunate enough to be rescued before their vessel sank. Other boats were later found drifting empty, the crews swept overboard from the decks. Some had been driven towards the Dutch coast and wrecked on the dangerous

A view of Barking Town Quay in 1924. LBBD Archives at Valence House Museum

sandbanks (or 'shoals') that lay there. Numerous seamen perished of cold and exhaustion. They had been pumping water out constantly in an attempt to keep their vessels afloat.

The crews of many ships, seeing others in danger of sinking, made valiant rescue attempts. Some launched small lifeboats and risked their lives rowing across the tempestuous sea towards their stricken comrades. Getting the half-frozen rescued men out of the lifeboats and up into safety was also very difficult. Ropes had to be thrown down for them to knot around their waists so that they could be hauled up, and some rescuers had their arms broken.

One remarkable story of survival was that of the 72-ton *Thomas & Edward*, belonging to James Morgan. The master's name was Jennings, the

Model of the Barking fishing smack 'Saucy Jack'. Valence House Museum

mate was Regan, and the seamen were Mitchell and Pelton. The crew was supplemented by three apprentice boys. The vessel was sixteen miles off the coast of Holland when it was hit by the storm. The crew lowered the anchors, but the ferocity of the winds caused the anchors and part of the chain to break away completely, leaving the boat tossing about at the mercy of the elements. The four men on board tried desperately to add ballast to the anchor chain, but one by one they were swept off the deck and into the savage sea.

The three boys, aged between thirteen and sixteen, were now left alone on board. Determined to carry on the work begun by their lost shipmates, they gathered as much iron ballast as they had strength to carry, and tied it to what remained of the anchor chain. One boy lashed himself to the tiller. Eventually the vessel was stabilized, thus keeping it steady in the face of the furious gale. Help came at last in the shape of a North Sea pilot who brought the *Thomas & Edward*, without serious damage, to the port of Emden in north-west Germany. *The Times* wrote approvingly: 'Saved by the presence of mind of a mere boy…This is the material which develops itself into the British seaman.'

A similar situation occurred on board the *Vulture*, owned by the Hewett brothers. Three apprentices survived, having been sent below decks, but its master, John Moss, mate, Edward Bellinger, and two seamen named Knight and Lincoln all perished. The *Vulture* was eventually towed into Yarmouth.

Remnants of the fishing fleet gradually made their way back to the east coast ports and eventually to Barking. Many craft had masts and rudders broken like sticks, and sails in tatters. The scene at Great Yarmouth was pitiful. Relatives and friends of the seamen gathered on the quay, searching for news and desperately scanning the horizon. Over sixty sailors had to be carried ashore and transferred immediately to beds at the Yarmouth Sailors' Home. A Government steamer, the *Medusa*, left Great Yarmouth on a search and rescue mission in the North Sea, hoping to pick up vessels drifting aimlessly because of damaged steering and sails. Gunboats from Harwich and Hull left on the same task, travelling round to the mouth of the River Elbe in search of the missing smacks.

News reached Barking that at least forty of its fishermen and boys had been lost, with the total expected to rise considerably. The rescued crew of the *Volante* were brought back to Barking on 12 December on board the *Samuel*. One man, William Patrick, had his ear cut off, and another, Alfred Cribb, had his arm dislocated and a leg badly injured. The *Essex Herald* reported that 'the whole crew appeared in a most pitiable state, and told too truly of the dreadful sufferings it had been their lot to endure'. The smack *Harry*, owned by James Morgan, had been towed into Hamburg a complete wreck. Three crewmen had drowned, including Waegman the mate, and the remainder arrived back in Barking on 15

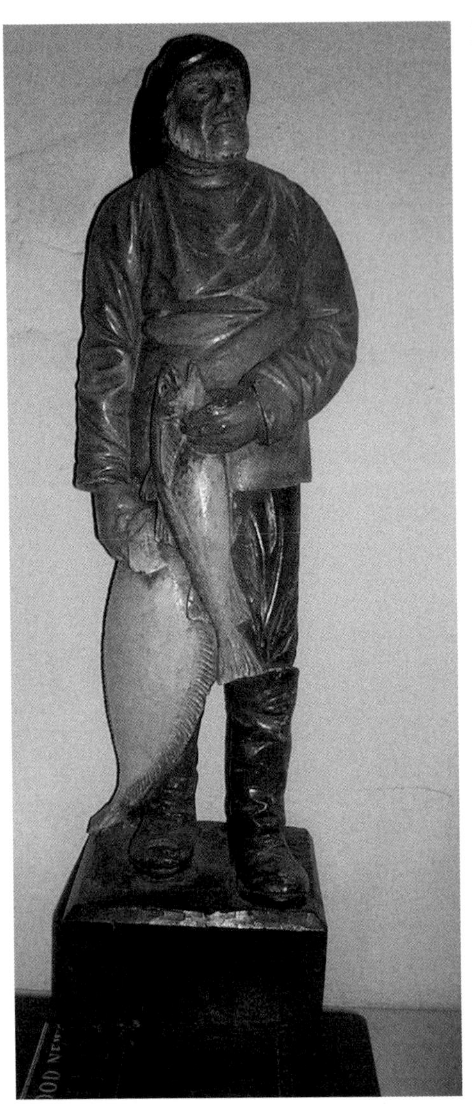

Figure of a fisherman inside St Margaret's Church, Barking.

December, the captain reportedly seriously injured. The surnames of other seamen whose deaths were confirmed included Bellinger and Lydia, master and mate of the *Prima Donna*; Abrahams, mate of the *Defiance*; Burrell and Montgomery, master and mate of the *Alpha*; Taw, mate of the *Ebenezer*; Priest, a seaman on board the *Leander*; and Sawyer, master of the *Marchant*.

The financial loss to shipping was also high, estimated at between £6,000-£7,000. The town's leading inhabitants quickly set up a relief fund for the many families now deprived of breadwinners. One of the prime movers in the campaign was Barking's vicar, the Reverend Henry Fortescue Seymour. As much money as possible was being collected in the town itself, but the vicar felt that the net should be spread wider. On 21 December he sat down in the vicarage in Ripple Road to write to *The Times*. Christmas was approaching, the time of year when charitable giving came to the fore, and he was determined that the spotlight should fall on the plight of Barking's countless widows and fatherless children.

The vicar's letter described the background to Barking's extensive fishing industry, then told of the destruction and loss of life wrought by the storm. He wrote that 'In one case, one little boy was found in the cabin, the only one left to tell the tale of shipwreck and death – while of those men who were fortunate enough to gain the shore, some are injured for life'. He invited *The Times* readers to think about those who risked their lives in order to provide the public with a staple food, 'what may almost be called a necessity of life'. He ended by hoping that his letter would 'arouse the sympathies of those who, fortunately for themselves, carry on their business and enjoy their pleasures far from the rolling sea'.

This was only the beginning. Seymour sent regular updates on the situation to *The Times* and other newspapers. He also published the names of all contributors to the relief fund, no matter how small the amount. Even anonymous donations were listed. This turned out to be a masterstroke. On opening their daily copy of *The Times*, relatively wealthy citizens such as Barking's many absentee landlords were spurred into action. If people of limited means, such as the employees of a Whitechapel tobacconist, banded together to raise ten shillings, or an anonymous 'Brother of a Fisherman' gave two shillings, then what would the public think if their own prominent names failed to appear? Large donations included £5 from the Marquess of Salisbury, whose family had long been associated with the town, and £20 from Sir Edward Hulse, Barking's Lord of the Manor.

Meanwhile, the agonizing wait continued for the fishermen's relatives. They must have clung to hope for weeks, imagining that their loved ones could be drifting on rudderless boats or washed up on some foreign shore. On 22 December the *Essex Herald* named four missing Barking vessels, the *Ann*, the *Diana*, the *Pursuit* and the *Ann & Elizabeth*. On Christmas Day, three weeks after the storm, the *Chelmsford Chronicle* reported that 'We are happy to learn that one of the missing Barking vessels, the *Pursuit*, has been heard of, and that the crew are all safe on board. We are, however, sorry to say that there is another vessel missing which has not been mentioned, viz. the *Antelope*, belonging to Mr J. Morgan'.

On New Year's Day, the Reverend Seymour wrote to *The Times* that 'The worst fears are realised with regard to the missing vessels. The Government steamer has returned with no tidings whatever of them'. The Barking death toll now stood at sixty and, on 12 January, he repeated his appeal for the 'relief of 29 widows and 54 orphans deprived of their natural protectors, and fallen suddenly from a state of comparative domestic comfort to apparently hopeless poverty'. He pointed out that many elderly men and women had also been left destitute, having formerly been supported by their sons. Donations continued to pour in from all levels of society. Help was also at hand from City of London merchants connected with Billingsgate Market, which was largely supplied by the Barking fishing fleet. By the middle of January they had collected £100.

On 25 January 1864, *The Times* stated that as a result of appeals in its columns over £1,400 had been raised to be divided between Yarmouth and Barking. Unfortunately, no complete list of names of the dead and missing was published. All of Barking's fishing families must have been affected in some way, losing relatives, neighbours or friends. It leaves a question mark down to the present day – family historians tracing Barking fishing fleet ancestors often find that they disappear from the records between the censuses of 1861 and 1871, leaving no death certificate or burial record. The cruel North Sea was their likely grave.

Sources

The Times
The *Essex Standard*
The *Chelmsford Chronicle*

Chapter 7

Neglected and Abused: Sad Tales of Fishing Apprentices

...he could hardly walk, but the cruel captain only laughed and had him tied up again.

It was traditional for British seafarers to begin their careers at a very early age. Horatio Nelson, for example, first went to sea at the age of 12. This was also the custom in the Barking Fishing Fleet, which was heavily reliant on its apprentice boys. Records show that many came from outside Barking. Often they were orphans or from poor families, parish vestries having willingly paid the required premiums to prevent the children becoming a burden to ratepayers.

The North Sea fishing ground was a harsh environment, especially in winter. In *Barking Vestry Minutes and other parish documents*, James Oxley writes that 'Thomas Moungall, fisherman, frequently took apprentices; he had a boy aged eight on 5 February 1767, and in July had another. One can only hope it was not to replace the earlier one, who may have died.'

St Nicholas, patron saint of fishermen and children. This figure inside St Margaret's church includes a Barking fishing smack at the base.

John Jones, 1827

Apprentices who refused to leave on a voyage could be prosecuted in the courts and sent to jail with hard labour. Yet the fate that awaited some of them at sea was sometimes even worse. In March 1827 12 year old John Jones was on board a Barking trawler named the *Rambler* in the North Sea. The captain was William Bowers, and his crew consisted of the mate, three seamen and three

A view of Barking Town Quay in 1907. LBBD Archives at Valence House Museum

boys. John and his fellow apprentices took care of menial tasks on board, such as coiling ropes, while listening out for the cry of 'Boy!' at which they had to drop everything and fetch and carry for the crew.

One day, when John happened to soil his shirt, William Bowers meted out a savage punishment. He bound the boy hand and foot to a windlass with his back exposed for six hours, and lashed him nine or ten times with a knotted whip. One of John's fellow apprentices, Richard Walsh, bravely untied the ropes and tried to help him get below deck. John said he could hardly walk, but the cruel captain only laughed and had him tied up again. The weather was bitterly cold. The mate, Joseph McQuay, gave Jones his cap and mittens, but the captain ordered them to be taken off him. A fellow apprentice brought him something to eat. When Jones was eventually freed and carried below deck, he was unable to speak and could scarcely move. He was placed near a fire and efforts made to revive him, but shortly afterwards he died.

The *Rambler* made her way back to Barking, where an inquest into the lad's death was held at the *Queen's Head* pub. *The Times*, scenting a scandal, sent a reporter, who managed to view the body, and was horrified: 'The back and loins were streaked with stripes of a livid gangrenous hue, as if occasioned by heavy flogging; and the breast, and other parts of the frame, exhibited several indications of serious external violence.'

The inquest jury appeared to see things differently, however. Six were smack-owners themselves, and one, a Mr Hughes, was the father-in-law of the owner of the *Rambler*. Two medical men called as witnesses stated that the boy's wounds 'were not mortal', and the jury's verdict was that Jones 'died from exposure to the weather'. Needless to say, they objected vehemently to the presence of *The Times* reporter at the hearing. The newspaper must have angered them even more by printing certain allegations from Jones's stepfather. He claimed that associates of William Bowers had tried to bribe him to withdraw the case – four guineas if all further enquiry was dropped, increased to ten guineas if he could ensure that the inquest proceedings were not published.

Joseph Morgan, 1844

Two decades later, a similar case of ill-treatment hit the headlines. In the summer of 1844 the Marine Society arranged for 16 year old Joseph Morgan and Joseph Bartlett, 14, to be apprenticed to William Smith, a Barking smack-owner who also ran the *Blue Anchor* pub in Heath Street. The two boys were said to be healthy and well-educated, and as well as paying their premiums the Marine Society had provided them with plenty of good clothing. In December 1844 Morgan and Bartlett sailed from Barking aboard the smack *Gem* towards fishing grounds off the coast of Holland. It was captained by a man named Howe, who had five crew plus the two apprentices.

One man on board, named James Naulls, reported that it was the worst weather he had ever experienced. For the apprentices, conditions were appalling. The warm clothes the Marine Society had provided had been taken away. They had nothing to wear but what were later described as 'a few old garments not fit to screen them from the severity of the weather, exposed as they necessarily must be in their calling in life'. They had no beds, and had to lie on damp worn-out nets with only a blanket and old rug to cover them, and no nightclothes to change into. There was no fire. Sometimes the master, Howe, kept them without food, saying they were lazy.

One day Howe lost his temper with Joseph Morgan and kicked him in the knee. When the lad limped to the cabin to rest, he was ordered back on deck. His injury became so bad that for the final four days of the voyage he could not walk at all. The day after the *Gem* returned to Barking, both Morgan and Bartlett were taken to a seamen's hospital ship, the *Dreadnought*. Morgan was now unconscious, and the doctor found marks of violence on his body. On his left thigh was a black bruise the size of a palm, apparently caused by repeated blows. His legs were also dreadfully swollen and frostbitten. Morgan was put to bed and given plenty of tea and diluted hot wine. His body and feet were wrapped in hot flannel and rubbed with turpentine. Unfortunately these efforts were to no avail, and Joseph Morgan died fifteen hours after being admitted to the *Dreadnought*.

An inquest into his death was held at the *Unicorn* tavern at Greenwich. Morgan's fellow apprentice Joseph Bartlett had recovered sufficiently to tell the jury of the ill treatment they had received on board the *Gem*. The vessel's owner, William Smith said there *were* beds for apprentices on his vessels. 'He defies any man to say the contrary… If any person has said there are none on oath, they have spoken falsely.' Smith praised the dead lad, saying that he 'was the best boy he had employed in his life'. The Coroner, however, was not impressed, and declared that Smith would be answerable for the lives of the boys. 'Dogs in a stable were treated with more humanity that his apprentices had been', he thundered. He stated he knew several members of the Marine Society who would be 'greatly surprised to learn such doings towards poor boys'.

The inquest jury were of the same mind. They reached a unanimous verdict that Morgan's death was a result of 'having been most inhumanely exposed to wet and cold, through want of proper care and attention, and also from want of the proper necessaries of life while on board the *Gem*'. The jurors stated they were sorry that the law did not allow for charges to be brought against both the master of the vessel, Howe, and its owner, Smith. According to the *Essex Standard*, 'they consider the conduct of owner and master highly criminal, and deserving severe punishment, which unfortunately was not in their power to inflict'.

Robert Hennekey, 1870

In late 1869 the Brentwood Board of Guardians paid for 16 year old Robert Hennekey to become an apprentice to a Barking smack owner named Mr Bass. Robert's first voyage passed without incident, and in March 1870, in good health and spirits, he left again for the North Sea on board the *Gnat*.

The captain of the *Gnat*, George Stiggles, injured his leg. His replacement, Charles Pigrome, was sent out to the vessel on one of the fast steamboats that by this time were used to collect the fish and take it to port. Arriving on board, Pigrome discovered that Robert Hennekey and another apprentice named Thomas Conway were in a bad state of health. He sent a letter via the steamer to Mrs Bass, who managed the business on behalf of her husband, telling her that in his opinion both boys were too ill to work. He wrote that Hennekey was covered in frostbites and sores, and asked her to send some gloves for him. Pigrome also requested extra crewmen.

A reply arrived three or four days later. Mrs Bass thundered 'I don't know what you mean. You must work yourself. As for the boys, you expect them all to be like men. You must not let them eat so much.' If he dared to bring the *Gnat* back early, she threatened to have him and the crew sent to prison as she had apparently done with the crew of another smack, the *Madcap*. Mrs Bass surely had much in common with the grotesque figure of Mrs Squeers in Dickens's *Nicholas Nickleby*.

So Robert Hennekey remained on board. One day he was sent down to the hold to coil a rope, and when he didn't reappear another boy was sent down after him. Hennekey was lying unconscious. He was immediately put to bed, but died the next morning. His body was brought to Yarmouth, and his fellow apprentice, Thomas Conway, was so ill that he too was brought ashore.

The inquest on Robert Hennekey was held at the *Guardian Angel*, Southtown, Norfolk. Mr Bass, owner of the *Gnat*, was in Yarmouth at the time but chose not to give evidence. Mr Arnott, a surgeon from Gorleston, said the cause of death was 'congestion of the lungs, from want of due circulation of blood in consequence of long exposure to cold'. He believed it was likely that if Hennekey had been given better clothing, he would not have died. Mr Arnott found no signs of violence on the body, nor any signs of starvation, but he reported that the boy's hands, arms, ankles and other parts of the body had huge boils, in their last stage, which had obviously not been attended to. Charles Pigrome, the relief captain, told the inquest that Hennekey's clothes were 'not fit to put on a mop stick'.

The letter from Mrs Bass was read out, and the Coroner, Mr C.H. Chamberlin, exclaimed 'Did you ever hear anything so abominable?' He told the jury that the letter was 'a most unfeeling and cruel one', but that he didn't believe the evidence justified a verdict of manslaughter. The jurors followed his advice, and returned an open verdict to the effect that 'death was accelerated by having insufficient clothing, and being exposed to the inclemency of the weather'. They added that they thought the owners were guilty of great neglect in not providing the boy with proper clothes. The *Essex Times* reported that the second apprentice, Thomas Conway, had recovered sufficiently to return to London, but that 'Mrs Bass has refused to have anything more to do with him'.

Most employers, even the most hard-hearted, would surely want their employees to be in good health so that they could get good productive work from them. However, because there was a constant supply of lads as fishing apprentices, requiring no wages but bringing premiums of up to £4 each, they seem to have been regarded as expendable. Many had no parents living, and nobody to complain on their behalf if they succumbed to the harsh conditions. Social campaigners spoke out against the abuse of child labour as chimney-sweeps, mineworkers and mill-workers, but many seemed unaware of the unfortunate boys suffering on fishing smacks far away at sea.

Sources

The *Chelmsford Chronicle*
The *Barking & Dagenham Recorder*
The Times
The *Essex Standard*

Chapter 8

Oh Fatal, Cursed Jealousy: Amelia Blunt 1864

...if you are in any part of England within a month you will see that I have had every drop of blood from her body.

Chadwell Heath derives its name from two sources: the settlement of Chadwell, meaning 'cold spring', and the open land to the north of the High Road formerly known as Blackheath Common. By the mid-1860s, rapid changes were occurring in the area. A railway had been driven through it back in 1839, but trains did not stop there until January 1864. The opening of the station put London within easy reach, and the area inevitably began to take on the character of a suburb. The heath itself was enclosed shortly afterwards, and a large portion sold off for brick-built terraced housing. Yet there still remained a few examples of the traditional 'small log cabins, thatched, one storey high', described by John Peter Shawcross. One of these wooden cottages could be found on the northern side of the heath, near the three post mills. In

The Old Mill Cottages on Chadwell Heath. Amelia Blunt would have lived in a similar wooden dwelling. LBBD Archives at Valence House Museum

September 1864 a 43 year old woman named Amelia Blunt sat inside, sewing her wedding dress.

Born Amelia Wallis in October 1820, and known to all as Milly, she had lived in Chadwell Heath most of her life. At 19 she had married Buckinghamshire-born John Blunt, but two of their four children, Elizabeth and Henry, both sadly died in infancy. In the 1850s the family moved to North London, but John Blunt was to die there at the end of the decade. Amelia then left her surviving children, Ellen and Margaret, with relatives while she returned to Chadwell Heath and supported herself by taking in washing.

One of Amelia's friends from childhood was Francis Wane, known as Toddy, an agricultural labourer eighteen months her junior. He had never married, and lived at Wood Lane, Dagenham, with his widowed father. Wane and Amelia rekindled their friendship, and by 1861 they were living together in lodgings near the Chadwell Heath Post Office. Wane was a powerful man, over 6 feet tall, and well known to the police as a drunkard and convicted thief. He did not treat Amelia well. According to *The Times*, 'He seems to have mainly subsisted upon the produce of her labour, and when drunk was constantly in the habit of ill-using her'. Amelia remained with Wane for over three years, before finally deciding to leave him in June 1864. She then obtained the post of housekeeper to 78 year old James Warren, known by all as Old Warren, who lived with his son John, 49, in the ancient cottage on the heath. Amelia also worked part-time as a cleaner at the *White Horse* pub, on the High Road. She had known the Warren family all her life, and not long after becoming their housekeeper she and John Warren decided to marry.

Amelia's former lover took this news very badly. Towards the end of August 1864 Joseph Rogers, a dealer in government stores from Spitalfields, stopped at the *White Horse* on his way home from Romford Market. Francis Wane offered to mind his horse and trap, so Rogers brought him out some bread, cheese and a pint of porter. Something in Wane's manner made Rogers ask 'What is the matter with you? You need not be afraid of telling me, for I am a man that has seen a great deal of the world.' Wane replied 'Now Master, I will tell you. I have been looking a month for a woman as I want her blood.' Rogers replied 'For God's sake, do not think of such a deed!' Wane answered 'So help me God, I have sworn to do it, and do it I will'. Rogers urged him to reflect on what he had said, 'Perhaps in time you will think better of it'. On parting, he gave Wane three pence and pleaded 'May God turn your heart', but Wane's reply was 'No, guv'nor – if you are in any part of England within a month

The White Horse *pub. Amelia Blunt and Francis Wane drank here, and it was the scene of heated arguments between them.* LBBD Archives at Valence House Museum

you will see that I have had every drop of blood from her body'. Wane then indicated the handle of a large knife protruding from his side pocket.

About a week later, Amelia was drinking in the *White Horse* with her future father-in-law James Warren and his grandson, also named James. Wane approached her, and pleaded 'Is there any chance for you and I to come together again?' She replied 'No, there never will, Toddy. You had a chance of having me for a wife, but you didn't use me well and you broke my home up, so I shall never have anything more to do with you.' He then growled 'Milly, you will have to die', to which she answered 'If I die, Toddy, you'll have to die too'.

Charles Fitch, landlord of the *White Horse*, was well used to Wane's behaviour, but shortly after this scene he finally lost his patience. He overheard Wane swearing at Old Warren about Amelia, and said to him 'Wane, you are like the dog in the manger, you won't live with a woman and you won't let her live peaceably with anyone else'. Wane swore in reply, and threatened to punch Fitch's head, so Fitch banned him from the premises 'on account of his quarrelling with Old Warren and his abusive language generally'. Wane switched his custom to another pub, the *Cooper's Arms*, close to where he had formerly lived with Amelia.

Wane entered the *Cooper's Arms* at 7.45 a.m. on Saturday, 24 September 1864. Amelia happened to be shopping nearby, and on passing the pub she saw a woman friend coming out. The pair stood outside chatting about Amelia's forthcoming marriage, and the jealous Wane overheard every word. Amelia then walked back to the cottage and got the dinner ready. Her next task was to do the washing. She lit a fire under the copper, a large cast-iron tub built into the corner of the lean-to washhouse, and proceeded to boil, scrub and beat the clothes by hand. It was arduous and thirsty work. After a while Amelia called out to old James Warren to go to the *White Horse* and fetch her some beer. He was happy to oblige, and left the cottage between 10.15 a.m. and 10.30 a.m. clutching the two pence halfpenny she had given him to pay for a pint of 'half and half'. Amelia's fiancé John Warren was out at work. On his way, the old man stopped at his grandson's house. They spoke of the coming marriage – the banns had now been read twice at Dagenham Parish Church – and 'how comfortable they would be'.

The beer was duly purchased, and within half an hour of leaving the cottage Old Warren was back at the front door. He called out 'Milly, here's your beer, girl, come and have it!' There was no answer. He went inside, put the beer on the table and sat down. She didn't appear, so he went to the door again and shouted 'Milly, are you coming?' Again there was silence, so he made his way towards the washhouse. On entering he saw Milly from behind, standing and leaning forwards against the copper as if in the act of taking clothes out. Her left arm lay on the copper, while the other rested on a sieve containing some potatoes. Her head was bowed over her hands. 'Milly, why won't you give me an answer?' he asked, but she said nothing and did not move.

As Warren came closer, he could see that blood was oozing from Amelia's neck and her hair was greatly disordered. He cried 'Milly, old girl, what's the matter with you?' and put his arms around her waist to try to raise her up. His hands felt wet and slippery. He managed to lift her up but she fell backwards on top of him. The old man stumbled under her weight and they both fell to the floor. He thought he heard her groan once. He fainted, and on regaining consciousness he became aware of warm blood trickling through his fingers.

Warren pulled himself up and rushed towards the home of his closest neighbours, Thomas and Frances Archer. The Archer children saw him first, and ran to their mother, crying 'Mr Warren has come down, something has happened at his house'. Mrs Archer went out to meet him, to be told 'Good God, Milly Blunt has fallen down dead!' They went to raise the alarm.

Charles Fitch, landlord of the *White Horse*, was playing with one of his children in the pub garden when he heard raised voices. His wife called out to him that 'poor old Milly' had dropped dead. Fitch immediately went to

Warren's cottage, and on seeing the body he exclaimed 'Bless me, the woman has been murdered!' Fitch sent someone to alert the police, then borrowed the local butcher's horse and cart and set out for medical help.

Before long he spotted Romford surgeon Robert Bowers, and brought him back at about 11.30 a.m. Bowers entered the washhouse and saw Amelia lying on her left side on the floor in a large pool of blood. There were three terrible wounds in her throat and on the right side of her neck, 'One transverse, another running obliquely from this one, a third just above the right collarbone. All of which were cut deeply, dividing the muscles of the carotid artery. I put my finger into the two first-named wounds and touched the vertebrae of the neck.' Amelia's left thumb was cut above the knuckle as if she had raised it to try to defend herself, and part of the brickwork surrounding the copper had been torn away by her as she tried to get away from her attacker.

PC Thomas Dunmow was already on the scene, and together with PC Thomas Cole and Old Warren's grandson James, he made a close examination of footprints in a freshly-ploughed field between about twenty to twenty-five yards from the cottage. They were unusual prints in that the right foot showed no mark of a heel and only the faint impression of a toe. Francis Wane was now the prime suspect as he had peculiar short, almost club feet, and only trod on the side of his right foot. The trio followed the prints in a northerly direction for about three quarters of a mile across freshly-ploughed land to Rose Lane, in Marks Gate. They spoke to a farm worker who told them he had seen Wane cross a meadow belonging to Warren Farm. They set off in pursuit, and the prints soon reappeared. A little further on they reached a pond, and noticed the same footprints in the clay beside it, and on the edge were marks indicating that someone wearing corduroy trousers had been kneeling down.

About a quarter of a mile further on, they spotted Wane himself about 150 or 200 yards from them. He came out of a ditch, turned round and looked at PC Dunmow, then got over the hedge and went into a wood known as Leigh's Wood, about a mile from the boundary with the parish of Romford. Dunmow followed, and about ten yards inside the wood he found Wane concealed under some blackberry bushes. Dunmow knew Wane well and greeted him familiarly. 'Hello Toddy, you must get up, I want you'. Wane wouldn't budge, so the officers pulled him up. Dunmow asked 'Do you know your old sweetheart had been murdered by someone?' Wane made no answer, and Dunmow demanded 'Were you on Chadwell Heath this morning?' Wane said he had visited the *Cooper's Arms*. Had he been to Warren's cottage that morning? Wane said he had not.

Wane was wet up to the waist, and there were spots of blood on the left shoulder of the jacket and also his plaid waistcoat. The cuffs of his jacket sleeves and part of his waistcoat had been torn off. His boots corresponded exactly with the footprints, and were filled with water. Wane had no cap, and the officers found no knife on him. PC Dunmow announced he was taking Wane into custody on suspicion of murdering Mrs Blunt. The time was now about 12.15 p.m. The policemen escorted their prisoner to Warren's cottage and showed him Amelia's body. Someone present said he 'could not touch the poor creature', to which Wane snarled 'I could touch her forty ___ times'. He was then taken to Ilford Police Station.

Later that afternoon PC Dunmow, along with Sergeant Samuel Maddison, followed the footprints again, and found a knife hidden in some grass not more than twenty yards from the cottage. It was a rather rusty pig-killing knife, with a six-inch blade and wooden handle, wet with blood and with a dark human hair stuck to it. Towards evening James Bell, a labourer at Warren Farm, was raking a pond near the cottage when he disturbed a brick, and Wane's missing cap rose to the surface. Had it been used to wipe blood off his trousers, and then thrown in the water? Two days later, on Monday morning, the cuffs of Wane's jacket were found in a meadow opposite Warren Farm. One was drenched in blood, and there were spots of blood on the other.

The inquest opened that same day, Monday, at the *White Horse*, only to be adjourned. It resumed two days later at the Petty Sessions Room at Ilford Gaol before Charles Carne Lewis, the Coroner, and a jury of local men of whom Archer Moss, miller, was foreman. The proceedings lasted over five hours. Wane was present, and described by the *Chelmsford Chronicle* as 'a tall, masculine, thick set fellow, with a large head, [and] full face'. There was damning evidence from John Turner, a Romford labourer. At a little past 10 a.m. on Saturday 24th, Turner had seen Wane in a lane leading across the heath from the High Road to Marks Gate via the three mills. 'Halloa, Toddy', he had said, 'Ain't you at work?' After a short conversation Wane had said ominously 'If you will wait a little while you will soon hear that something is up'. They were close to a field farmed by Wane's brother. Wane entered it, stooped down, then picked up something from under a hedge and put it under his jacket. He then walked off in the direction of Warren's cottage. Two children, Martha Fenn and Emma Embery, then told the Coroner they had seen Wane go along the path leading to Warren's cottage.

James Warren the younger identified the knife. He said that it belonged to Wane's brother Thomas, and that Wane himself was in the habit of using it in trimming greens. Warren had also used it himself for this purpose when they worked alongside each other. Finally, two men named Thomas Hart and William Outtram were brought in. They shared a cell with Wane at Ilford Gaol, and told the inquest that he had confessed to the murder three or four times. He was apparently very sorry that it happened, and had wailed 'I shall be hung; I am sure to be hung… I don't think there is any chance of my getting off for they all surrounded me so I could not get away'. When asked how long Amelia had lived, he allegedly said 'She was not quite two minutes dying'.

Wane vehemently denied saying this. The inquest jury, however, did not take long to return a verdict of 'Wilful Murder' against him. Amelia was buried the same day at Dagenham Parish Church, where she had been baptized and married. On Saturday, 1 October Wane was brought before the Ilford magistrates. The *Chelmsford Chronicle* reported that he 'surveyed those present with a defiant look…leaned his arms on front of the dock, and on several occasions he asked the witnesses questions in a bullying tone'. When Joseph Rogers recounted what Wane had said to him outside the *White Horse*, we are told that Wane's face 'became black with passion, and he shouted vehemently "You are an infernal liar – you are merely giving evidence expecting to make a few shillings out of it".' John Warren was called, and told the magistrates that he was to have been married to Amelia that very day.

Wane's trial took place two and a half months later, on 14 December 1864, at the Chelmsford Assizes. He pleaded not guilty. Joseph Rogers again told the story of his conversation with Wane. When asked why he didn't report it to the police, he replied: 'Of what use would it be? I have often told the police such things, and they have said, "Oh, don't bother us, let them do as they like"…I can assure you the police are very lazy in London.' At this, the courtroom erupted into laughter. Wane's defence counsel Mr Woollett asked the jury to consider whether Amelia may have committed suicide. He also suggested that Wane was not a rational being. 'Did anyone hear of a man intending to murder, and telling the whole world of it?'

The jury retired, and about twenty minutes later returned and pronounced a verdict of guilty. Wane seemed unconcerned, but immediately after being removed to the cells below, his indifference and apathy melted away. He was full of emotion, and told the chief warder 'I did it, and I was sure they would bring me in guilty'. Wane explained that he thought Amelia was going to be married the following day, Sunday, 25 September. He had silently entered the washhouse and put his left arm around her neck. She spun round, and with a look of horror, exclaimed 'Oh, Toddy, what do you do here?' Without a word of reply, he had immediately cut her throat with a knife held in his right hand. Wane told the governor of Springfield Gaol that 'I had the thoughts on me for months that I must do it, and I struggled with them over and over again; but it was no use, they were too much for me'.

Wane's execution was fixed for Wednesday, 28 December. He was placed in the condemned cell and watched night and day. He complained bitterly of the cold, and the governor had two cells prepared for him, one for day and one for night, installed with a hot-water heating apparatus. On 26 December Wane's eldest brother and brother-in-law visited him, the only family members to do so. Wane asked the governor to write to his other brother, and entreat him to beware of 'the drink', declaring it had brought this terrible fate upon him. On Tuesday evening he dictated this letter:

> *My dear father, I write to you bidding you goodbye, as I shall not see you again in this world, but I hope we shall meet again in Heaven. May God Almighty bless you. Dear father, I was guilty of the crime with which I am charged…Accept my kind love, and give the same to the rest of the family.*

On Tuesday evening two prisoners were ordered to dig the grave of the still-living man deep within the confines of the prison. The hangman William Calcraft, who had executed Charles Saunders at the same place eleven years before, arrived at 5 p.m. and spent the night at the gaol. Two people had contacted the governor offering to undercut Calcraft's fee. One wrote that he would carry out the execution for a mere £5 plus railway expenses. At 4 a.m. on Wednesday the carpenters started to put up the gallows over the entrance gate. The prison's passing bell tolled mournfully.

Wane had spent a very restless night, and from an early hour he knelt in prayer with the chaplain. He was very nervous and tremulous at first, throwing himself from side to side and wailing that he was going mad, but as the time advanced he grew calmer. He gave the chaplain a little book called *Cottage Hymns* to be sent to his niece. Wane dreaded the thought of being brought out before the crowd, and said he 'should not have thought so much of it if it had been private'. He complained that 'the punishment is too great, it is too hard'.

A few minutes before 9 a.m. Wane was escorted across the yard and up the steps into a room where the hangman waited. Here, however, his courage seemed to fail him, and he became very agitated. He was offered a glass of brandy – the final tipple of a lifetime of drinking – which was gratefully accepted. Calcraft then proceeded to pinion Wane's arms, and he winced as this was being done, exclaiming 'Don't hurt me!' The chief warder then helped Wane ascend the steps leading to the scaffold, while the chaplain read out the burial service. Standing on the trapdoor, the condemned man trembled very much and looked ghastly pale. After Calcraft had placed the noose around his neck, and drawn the cap over his face, the crowd fell silent. People directly in front of the gaol could clearly hear Wane cry out 'Lord Jesus, have mercy on me! Oh Lord, have mercy on my soul!' In a few moments the drop fell, and he appeared to die almost immediately.

About 1,500 spectators had come to witness the execution, which was to be the penultimate public hanging at Chelmsford. According to the *Chelmsford Chronicle* the atmosphere resembled a country fair, with people smoking, laughing and chatting. Immediately the drop fell, 'a decent-looking countryman was heard to declare, with a fearful oath, that he wouldn't mind seeing a thousand of 'em hung, or hanging them himself for that matter'. Groups of open-air preachers and Temperance Society tract distributors were at the scene, lecturing the crowd 'to take warning by the fate of the wretched criminal, to beware of drink and put a curb upon their passions'.

The murder of Amelia Blunt was the subject of a popular ballad, beginning:

Behold a sad and wretched man,
On Springfield's gallows high,
I a murder did on Chadwell Heath,
And for the same I die…

Oh! Fatal, cursed jealousy,
'Tis then that was the cause,
Of this most dreadful tragedy.

The writer, of course, correctly gives jealousy as Wane's motivating factor, but it also seems clear that poor Amelia was tragically let down by people's failure to take seriously Wane's repeated threats against her life.

Sources

Depositions (National Archives, ASSI 36/11)
The *Chelmsford Chronicle*
The *Essex Standard*
The ballad is quoted in an article by Roly Brown, *Glimpses into the 19th century broadside ballad trade* at http://www.mustrad.org.uk/articles/bbals_14.htm

Chapter 9

Till Death Us Do Part

I spoke to her but she did not answer.
She gave three breaths and then died.

Sarah Ann Bacon, 1867

On 12 April 1863 Sarah Ann Hopes, aged 20, entered St Edward's Church in Romford Market Place for her marriage to 21 year old James Bacon. They had both been brought up in Ilford, and decided to set up home there. In the summer of 1865, just over two years after their marriage, they moved to Aldborough Cottages on the Ilford High Road, near the *Cauliflower* pub and backing onto the Great Eastern Railway line. James Bacon was employed by a local farmer, George Butler, and proved to be very industrious and reliable. He was given the responsibility of buying and selling crops at market on behalf of his employer, and was soon earning £1 per week, a relatively high wage for an agricultural worker. Many young women also undertook farm work to bring in extra money, but James refused to allow Sarah to toil in the fields. He told friends he loved his wife so much that he 'doted on the ground she walked'. In July 1864 Sarah gave birth to a daughter named Emma Maria, and another baby girl, Alice, followed in November 1865. Both were christened at St Mary's Church, just a few minutes' walk west along the High Road from Aldborough Cottages.

So far, the couple's married life had been perfectly happy and unremarkable, but towards the end of 1866 Sarah's behaviour changed. She lost interest in caring for herself and her home, and neglected the children so much that even her own mother commented that 'they were hardly fit to touch'. To make things worse, Sarah was also frittering away the money that James gave her to pay the household expenses. At the beginning of March 1867 he came home from work and went upstairs to change, only to find that his clothes had disappeared. Sarah admitted she'd taken them to the pawnshop. But where was the money going? Her husband and her mother, who lived with them for a while, agreed that she wasn't spending it on drink.

Aldborough Cottages, High Road, the former home of James and Sarah Bacon. London Borough of Redbridge Local Studies/Mrs D. Lockwood

James Bacon arrived home at six o'clock on Saturday, 23 March 1867 after a hectic day at market. This would be a busy weekend for him, as he was due to leave for Chelmsford the following afternoon on business for his employer that would take several days. Any thoughts he may have had of a tranquil Sunday morning were, however, to be rudely shattered. A knock at the door resulted in a lawyer's letter being handed over on behalf of their landlord Mr Ashmole. Twenty-five shillings was owing in rent and the Bacons were given four days' notice to quit.

This was a staggering blow to James, who had always given Sarah the rent money promptly every Monday morning. Sarah then admitted that as well as the rent bill she had run up a much larger debt at a nearby shop run by Mrs Caroline Dowsett. A violent quarrel followed, overheard by their fellow lodgers Thomas and Emma Price. Eventually the shouting ceased and James went into the back yard. Emma Price then sought Sarah out. Shaking and crying, Sarah told her 'He ran after me with a chopper. I thought it would be my end, that he was going to kill me'.

Sarah had a cousin named Caroline Johnson who, with her husband William, had signed as witnesses to the Bacons' wedding four years before. The two young couples had remained close, so James and Sarah travelled early that Sunday afternoon to the Johnsons' home at Collier Row to seek their advice. James told of his fear that bailiffs would seize his furniture and property, but reassuringly William replied 'Never mind, Jim, so long as I live you shall not be at a loss for house room or a covering over your head. There is the back part of our house if that is any use to you'. The Bacons gratefully accepted the offer, and it was agreed that Sarah would move their things the five miles to the Johnsons' home the following Wednesday morning. James then left to take the train from Romford to Chelmsford, where he would be staying at the *Two Brewers* pub for a few days while engaged in buying turnip-tops for the London market.

Wednesday, 27 March dawned, the day arranged for the removal from Ilford to Collier Row. Sarah's hopes of slipping away quietly were foiled. A bailiff appeared and threatened to seize the furniture if the outstanding rent owed to Mr Ashmole was not paid. Sarah, unsurprisingly, had no money, but her aunt Isabella Stephens, Caroline's mother, stepped in to negotiate on her behalf with the landlord. Eventually he agreed to reduce his demand to 5s 6d, and in order to raise this sum Sarah sold a table to Mrs Dowsett, the shopkeeper. This lady then promptly served Sarah with an official demand of her own for the huge sum of £6, but appears to have granted Sarah time in which to pay.

It was then too late in the day to move the goods as planned, so Sarah and her children stayed at Aldborough Cottages one final night. The following morning, Thursday, 28 March, she and Isabella Stephens hired a horse and cart and loaded it with the Bacons' worldly goods. Shortly before 8 a.m. Sarah and her small daughters waved goodbye to her aunt as the cart moved off. They drove along the Ilford High Road, took Barley Lane to Little Heath, then Billet Lane to Marks Gate, finally reaching Caroline's house at Collier Row. Sarah unloaded the goods and then, at about 10.30, set off back to Ilford to return the horse and cart, finish a few jobs in her former house and hand back the key. Caroline had to leave at 1 p.m. to go to work at nearby Rose Lane Farm. A neighbour, Mrs Harriet Hoy, was left in charge of the Bacon children. She noticed that they were 'very dirty indeed, vermin on both'. The poor little ones were infested with lice and fleas.

That same morning James Bacon had finished his business in Chelmsford and set out on the journey home, taking the train to Romford. On leaving the station just after midday he recognized a friend, Edward 'Teddy' Pepper, who lived in Marks Gate. The pair walked from Romford to Collier Row together, then stopped off at *The Bell* pub for a pint. Bacon confided to Teddy about Sarah's debts, and told him he didn't know what to do next.

At about 1.15 p.m. they reached Caroline Johnson's house and James knocked on the door. Harriet Hoy opened it, holding the 16 month old Alice in her arms. She called out to Emma, aged 2, 'Here's your father, dear'. James took the baby from her, kissed it, and sat down. Mrs Hoy asked him if he wanted a cup of tea and he answered 'No, not yet'. She said she would boil the kettle so that he and Sarah could have tea together. James asked where Sarah was, and was told she had gone back to Ilford to return the key. 'What's the reason she didn't get here yesterday?' he demanded. Harriet explained what had happened, and Bacon cried out 'Oh, the bitch! I've had enough this last month for a horse to bear!' He jumped up, handed back the baby, and strode off to the nearby *Sun* pub. Not long afterwards he returned to the house and went upstairs to change his clothes. On coming down he asked Mrs Hoy whether she knew from which direction Sarah would come. She didn't, so he said 'Well, I'm going as far as Chadwell Heath, and perhaps I will meet her'. He kissed his children, bade them goodbye and left.

Bacon's destination was another pub, the *Old Marks Gate* in Whalebone Lane. When he reached it, his mood had not improved. According to the landlady, Mrs Sarah Brown, Bacon 'appeared to be in a very excited state' and offered his fellow drinkers five shillings 'to cut his own head off in one stroke'. When his friend Teddy Pepper arrived, James told him 'I've a great mind to leave my wife for a month or two. I'm having a great bother with her.' The two men had a few beers together, then stood talking outside the pub. James kept looking about in all directions, and eventually at about 2.45 p.m. he spotted Sarah approaching along Billet Lane. He said to Teddy 'I want a word or two with her', and strode off. The couple were seen to meet at the junction of Whalebone Lane and Billet Lane. They then walked away out of sight in the direction of Collier Row.

Pepper returned to the taproom, and about a quarter of an hour later he looked up to see Bacon at the door. There was blood on his hands and clothes, and he announced 'I'll give myself up to you, Teddy, I've been killing my wife'. His friend answered 'Nonsense, Jemmy, you don't mean to say so'. Bacon repeated 'I've murdered her. You'll find it true, and the knife and belt you will find lying by her side down where I've done it.' He downed another glass of ale. He then turned to the landlady, Sarah Brown, but she didn't believe him either. 'Govern your temper!' she snapped, and Bacon retorted that his temper had nothing to do with it. 'Think of your poor children', she told him, and he answered 'My children are my study, I do think of them. Well, if you won't take me, I'm going straight off to Chadwell to give myself up.'

Meanwhile, a man named Walter Fitch was driving a cart and two horses along the road between the pub and Collier Row when he caught sight of a woman staggering along, holding her hands up to her head. When he drew closer he noticed that her face and hands were covered with blood. Fitch stopped, and said 'Dear me, missus, you look in a very bad state, what's the matter with you?' Sarah wailed 'Oh, dear me!' and collapsed onto the grass. Fitch promised he would find somebody to help her as soon as possible, and drove on.

The first building he reached was the *Old Marks Gate*. James Bacon had left it a couple of minutes previously, having walked off in the opposite direction towards Chadwell Heath. When Fitch announced that 'There is a poor woman down the road who wants help', Mrs Brown and Teddy Pepper immediately dashed to the scene. They soon spotted some objects at the side of the road. These proved to be a bag of groceries – tea, butter, bread and some herrings – and, to their horror, a clasp knife 'open and bloody' lying close to its belt and holder. About 100 yards further on, just as the road curved to the right towards the National School, Mrs Brown saw Sarah:

She was lying on her left side, her hands stretched out. She was alive. I spoke to her but she did not answer. She gave three breaths and then died. There was blood on her face and shawl.

Meanwhile, Sarah's husband made his way as promised to Chadwell Heath Police Station and announced to Sergeant James Blain 'I've come to give myself up'. 'What for?' asked the officer. 'For wounding my wife. I've done it. I'm willing to suffer for it'. Bacon explained where he had left Sarah, and he was put in the custody of PC Jonathan Streames while Blain departed for Marks Gate. Bacon burst out crying, and said to Streames 'I hope to God I haven't killed her'. The sympathetic constable tried to reassure him, saying 'You mustn't look at the worst side of things'. Bacon answered 'No, but I'm afraid of it, as I used the knife to her'. Streames took Bacon into his living quarters. The prisoner asked for a glass of ale, but this was refused. Mrs Harriet Streames made him some tea, which he drank, but he refused food, saying he was 'too full of trouble to eat anything'. Bacon, though admitting what he had done, tried to justify it. 'It is a bad job; she caused me to do it by contracting debts unknown to me.'

When Sergeant Blain reached the spot where Sarah lay, her shawl had been placed over her face. He found on the body a pawn ticket for a waistcoat pledged for half a crown. At about 5 p.m. the surgeon Alfred Wright arrived. He made a cursory examination at the scene, followed by a detailed post-mortem two days later. He discovered a wound about an inch wide and three inches deep on the left side of Sarah's neck. It passed through her throat towards the opposite ear, cutting through the carotid artery and jugular vein. In his opinion, 'the knife had been thrust in the throat and drawn out at once'. She had then bled to death.

Blain returned to Chadwell Heath and got a horse and cart ready to take James Bacon to Ilford Police Station. On seeing him, the prisoner asked 'Is she dead?' and was told that yes, indeed she was. The news was broken to Sarah's mother, Elizabeth Hopes, in a shocking manner. Walking along the Ilford High Road that evening, she overheard someone say 'Oh dear, what a dreadful thing – Jim Bacon's killed his wife'. She went straight to the station but the officers refused to let her see James. Caroline Johnson reluctantly took his little daughters to the Romford Union Workhouse.

The following morning, Friday, Bacon was brought before a magistrate at Stratford. He was described in the press as 'a fine-built young man with nothing repulsive in his appearance'. The inquest into Sarah's death was held the next day at the *White Horse* in Chadwell Heath. The Coroner, Charles Carne Lewis, was appalled by her poverty-stricken appearance. 'I never saw a more miserable state in my life; she had nothing on but an old bit of a chemise, an old petticoat, and this miserable dress that is spattered with blood.'

Bacon was committed for trial at the next Essex Assizes and, on 20 July, he was duly escorted into the dock. Again, the press coverage was sympathetic. The *Chelmsford Chronicle* reported that 'The prisoner, a fine young man, who at first betrayed not the slightest emotion, pleaded Not Guilty in a loud, firm voice'. His defence counsel Mr Serjeant Parry was to argue that the killing arose from a sudden impulse, was not premeditated, and was thus a case of manslaughter. Most agricultural labourers, he stated, carried such a knife on them to cut up their lunch of bread, cheese and onion.

When the prosecution barrister began by describing to the jury the 'affectionate terms on which the prisoner had for a long time lived with his wife', Bacon's self-control left him. Leaning over the rail of the dock, he wept bitterly. A chair was brought, and he 'remained sitting during the greater part of the trial, with his face buried in his hands'.

Bacon's mother-in-law, Elizabeth Hopes, maintained that he was 'a good husband and very fond of his children', and this was backed up by several other witnesses. The defence called the vicar of Great Ilford, the Honourable Henry William Bertie, to the stand. He stated that:

> *I have known the prisoner for 20 years. He has always been quiet, orderly, industrious and well-conducted. I have always considered him of more than usually mild and kindly disposition, and it is not my testimony alone, but that of every one who knows him.*

After ten minutes' deliberation the jury announced their verdict – guilty of murder, adding 'With a strong recommendation to mercy on account of his previous strong character'. Bacon showed no emotion, and when asked if he wanted to say anything before the mandatory death sentence was passed, he calmly replied 'I have nothing to say, Sir'. The judge, Mr Baron Martin, then put on the black cap and, weeping as he spoke, pronounced the dreaded sentence of death by hanging. Bacon, unperturbed, bowed respectfully to the judge and jury, said 'Thank you gentlemen', and walked quietly from the dock.

Bacon's family was well-known in the Ilford area. His father, also called James, was a market gardener at Ley Street. The inhabitants of Ilford, led by the vicar and churchwardens, had already rallied round by paying for the services of the defence barrister, and their support continued after the verdict. A 250-signature petition was sent to the Home Secretary appealing against the death sentence. On 1 August, twelve days after the trial, news came through that it had been commuted to ten years' penal servitude. The *Chelmsford Chronicle* commented that 'We are sure that all who heard or read the trial will agree with us that there never was a case of the kind more deserving of a lenient and merciful consideration'.

James Bacon was sent to Dartmoor Prison, reckoned to be the most severe in England. His daughters Emma and Alice, meanwhile, were removed from the Romford Workhouse and cared for by their grandparents James and Maria Bacon. Bacon was eventually released on licence in March 1875. He remarried, and settled in Streatham with his second wife Mary Ann, children Emma and Alice and stepdaughter Rose. Bacon now earned a living as an itinerant greengrocer. Yet there was one further calamity in store. In April 1887 Bacon hanged himself in his stable. He was 45 years old.

Looking back at this tragic tale, two questions arise. Firstly, what could have caused Sarah to become incapable of looking after her home, children and finances properly, thus setting in motion the chain of events that would lead to her death? To modern eyes it suggests some form of mental illness. Could she have been suffering from delayed post-natal depression after the birth of her second child? Secondly, we must wonder why there was such an outpouring of sympathy for her murderer. James had, after all, admitted to stabbing Sarah in the neck. He must have known this was likely to kill her. By failing to carry out properly the wifely role expected of her, was poor Sarah viewed as a threat to the Victorian family, and therefore to the smooth running of society as a whole?

Bertha West, 1912

Forty-five years later, a similar case was to occur. In November 1911 a married couple moved into lodgings at 15 Station Road, Ilford. Tom West, aged 51 and born in Bow, was a railway boilermaker. His wife Bertha, formerly Richards, was a year older and came from Chepstow in Wales. The pair, married since December 1883, had three daughters and had lived at Forest Gate before moving to Ilford.

Their landlady, Elizabeth Painter, soon became aware of tensions within the West household. Bertha was a heavy drinker and liked to spend evenings in local pubs without her husband. Her eldest daughter Margaret, now married to Albert Rulten and with children of her own, grew worried about the welfare of Bertha's youngest child Lilian, 11, and took the girl into her own home. In the spring of 1911 Bertha had become friendly with a man named Alfred Faulkner, who lived at Railway Terrace,

A modern view of the Cooper's Arms, *scene of the killing of Bertha West.* Authors' collection

Laburnham Grove, Ilford. When she moved to Ilford the pair began to meet regularly. On the night of 23 December 1911 Bertha failed to return home, and it emerged that she had slept at Faulkner's house. She denied they were having an affair, but her relationship with her husband deteriorated and they argued constantly.

On the evening of Saturday, 6 January 1912 Mrs Painter asked Tom West for that week's rent. He replied that he had given the cash to his wife, who had left a few minutes before with her daughters Margaret and Lilian. They intended, he believed, to spend the evening at Margaret's house. He told the landlady he would follow and bring back the money. On reaching the house, he was told that Bertha had gone shopping, so he set off in search of her.

Bertha had, in fact, joined Alfred Faulkner in the *General Havelock* on Ilford High Road. They remained there about half an hour, then went to his house. There they poured more drinks and Faulkner took out his accordion. His serenade to Bertha was rudely interrupted when Tom West suddenly barged in and set about raining blows on Faulkner's head and face, while Bertha looked on helplessly. Faulkner put up no resistance, and less than a minute later his attacker left without saying a word.

Tom returned to his daughter's house at about 10 p.m. and told her he had given Faulkner a 'good hammering'. Shortly afterwards Bertha entered. The pair remained at Margaret's home for the next few days, Tom sleeping in the kitchen and Bertha upstairs. They hardly spoke to each other until Monday morning, when Tom asked if she wasn't ashamed of her conduct with Faulkner. Bertha replied indignantly that no, she wasn't ashamed as she'd done nothing wrong. She told her daughter that she enjoyed Faulkner's company and was determined to see him again.

Bertha had a job at a laundry on the Chadwell Heath High Road, and the following morning, Tuesday, 9 January, she left for work as usual. Just as she was about to start her lunch break Tom arrived, and they walked together to the nearby *Cooper's Arms*. He ordered a pint of beer and Bertha had a 'glass of ale with a dash'. They called for another round, and a little later Bertha stood up to go. Tom asked 'Why not stop here and have your dinner?' and she told him she'd brought her own lunch. Bertha then turned away, and the horrified barmaid Ethel Higgs saw Tom hit her behind the ear with what looked like his bare fist. Bertha immediately fell to the floor. Blood was pouring from a three-inch deep stab wound in her neck. Her husband refused to help pick her up, saying 'I have done it; let

The Shire Hall, Chelmsford, scene of Tom West's murder trial. Lee Shelden

her lie; I will answer for it'. He stood calmly nearby, smoking, while his wife's life ebbed away.

Tom West was put on trial for murder at the next Essex Assizes. Margaret Rulten explained that her father's hobby was shoe repairing, or 'snobbing,' and that the murder weapon was a knife he used in connection with this. She told the court that West had always been a good father to her. Alfred Faulkner was also summoned as a witness. He claimed that Bertha had never told him her husband objected to their meeting. He was 'sorry to say' that she had spent the night of 23 December at his house, but claimed it was entirely innocent – she had been 'the worse for drink' and incapable of leaving. He then alleged, somewhat to the amusement of the press and public, that when Tom West burst into his house on 6 January he had no idea who it was or why he was being assaulted. When asked whether he had reported the attack to the police, he said he hadn't, but 'it would have been better if I had'. He maintained that it was only by chance that he had met Bertha in the *General Havelock* that evening.

West's defence barrister Mr Salkeld Green did not call him to give evidence. He claimed that West's action could not be classed as murder because there had been 'not an atom of premeditation – it was the result of a sudden impulse'. The jury must have agreed, for after only thirty-five minutes' deliberation they returned a verdict of manslaughter. The judge told West that 'the jury have taken a very merciful view of your case. I cannot help thinking that it is a very serious offence, in which you are fortunate in not having a conviction against you on the charge of murder'. West was then sentenced to fifteen years' penal servitude. He was eventually released in April 1922, having spent ten years within the walls of Maidstone Jail.

Sources

Depositions (National Archives, ASSI 36/13)
The *Chelmsford Chronicle*
Lockwood, Herbert Hope: Murder most pitiful (*Ilford & District Historical Society newsletter*, January 1991)
The *Barking Advertiser*

Chapter 10

For Whom the Bell Tolls

There was no sign of her father, although she could hear someone groaning.

Parish churches often witnessed funerals of people who died in tragic circumstances. Yet occasionally the churches themselves were the scenes of shocking accidents.

Ringing the deadly changes

On 11 October 1804, *The Times* reported a melancholy accident which had happened the previous Saturday at the Parish Church of St Peter & St Paul at Dagenham. Back in December 1800 the church tower had collapsed onto the nave, fortunately without causing any injuries or deaths. By 1804 rebuilding work was complete, and the prestigious Society of Royal Cumberland Youths were invited to come down from London to open the new peal of bells. This they did on the morning of 6 October, ringing 7,008 changes of Oxford treble bobs royal in four hours and forty-nine minutes. According to *The Times*, however, 'in the evening, the master of the society wished to oblige the inhabitants of the village with another peal, when unfortunately his leg got entangled in the rope, which drew him to the next loft, and, falling on his head, he was killed on the spot.'

Unfortunately, almost seventy years later a very similar accident occurred at St Margaret's Church, Barking. The 1874 edition of *Kelly's Essex Directory*, describing the church, states that at the west end there is 'a lofty square embattled tower dating from the late 1400s and containing eight fine-toned bells, rung with great skill by the St Margaret's Campanological Society, composed of some of the principal tradesmen of the town.' One of the members of this society was 40 year old Henry Hall, a well-known figure in the town in his capacity as land and house agent, tax collector and bailiff to Sir Edward Hulse, Lord of the Manor. Durham-born Hall lived in Chestnut Villa in Queen's Road with his wife Annie and their three small children Amy, Annie and Harry. On Monday, 6 November 1871, having completed his day's work, Hall entered the

Dagenham Parish Churchyard under a fall of snow in 1962. LBBD Archives at Valence House Museum

Town Hall, a half-timbered building dating from Elizabethan times, situated near the Curfew Tower. Hall had an appointment with his fellow estate agent James Linsdell, who lived in Fisher Street, to go through the accounts of Barking Cricket Club. This took about an hour, after which they adjourned to the *Bull*, an ancient coaching inn on the Broadway, for some refreshment. Linsdell left shortly afterwards, saying he would see Hall later for the weekly bell ringing practice at St Margaret's.

At about 8.30 p.m. Hall stepped into the church and made his way up the narrow stone spiral staircase leading to the ringing chamber. One of the bells was broken, so only seven men were needed that evening. Their conductor, and ringer of the treble bell, was Robert Sewell, manager of Ridley's flour mill at the Town Quay. James Linsdell rang the sixth bell that evening, and Henry Hall the seventh. The group did about half a dozen rounds, then stopped and tied the ropes while they took a short break.

A new session then began. Another ringer present that evening, an East Street grocer named Alfred Carter, described what happened next. At about 9 p.m., on the fourth round of the new session, the heavy bell-rope swung behind Hall's legs, caught under the heel of one of his boots and flung him into the air. He turned upside down, then fell heavily on his left shoulder and the left side of his head. Hall lay face downwards, motionless. The others rushed to assist him. Carter stated that 'when we turned him over he asked for his hands and feet, and said he could not feel them'. Hall was conscious, and said he thought his arms were broken. He also begged them to hold his head up. Carter and the others rubbed Halls arms but they didnt seem to be damaged.

The injured man was plied with brandy while one of his fellow ringers ran for medical help. Within fifteen minutes Dr Francis Parsons of East Street was at the scene. He saw that the accident had left Hall totally paralysed and numb from the neck down, and knew that the man's neck must be broken. The group undertook the difficult task of manoeuvring Hall down the spiral staircase and out of the building. Placed on an airbed, he was carefully carried to his home in Queen's Road. His spinal cord was so severely damaged that the doctor could do nothing to help him, and he died at about 2 a.m. on Tuesday, five hours after the accident.

An inquest was held at the *Bull*, where Hall had enjoyed a drink on the fatal night. The coroner was Charles Carne Lewis Junior, and smack owner John Thomas Quash of Northbury House was foreman of the jury. James Linsdell maintained that he and Hall had not had much to drink

An early twentieth century postcard of St Margaret's Church, Barking. The outer stonework of the spiral staircase leading to the ringing chamber and roof turret can clearly be seen. Authors' collection

that evening, and 'there was no larking going on, as we were all too intent on improving our ringing, and there was only one man to each bell present'.

Carter told the jury that there was a handhold loop at the end of the rope. This had not been the cause of the accident, however, as the rope itself had curled under Hall's heel and thrown him over. A juror asked whether Hall had a habit of lifting his heel when ringing. Carter replied 'Yes, he used to beat time with his foot, which was a bad habit, and it was through the lifting of his foot that the rope got under it.' The conductor that evening, Robert Sewell, explained that Hall had a bad habit of lifting his foot, which I had spoken to him about before, though I never thought that such a thing as this resulting from it'. A verdict of accidental death was recorded, and Mr Quash suggested that a raised platform should be made in the ringing chamber to allow the rope to fall below and not remain near the feet of the ringers.

Henry Hall was brought back to St Margaret's to be buried in the churchyard. The inscription on his gravestone, which has now disappeared, read: 'Sacred to the memory of Henry Hall who was accidentally killed whilst bellringing in this church on the 6 November 1871.'

Buried alive, 1878

The Palmer family were prominent Dagenham farmers, tradesmen and publicans in Victorian times. A visitor to Dagenham parish churchyard looking closely at a memorial stone to them, situated close to the wall at the south-east corner, will notice that a member of the family met his end near that very spot in a particularly shocking manner.

In the early nineteenth century William Palmer was a carpenter living and working in the centre of the village. One of his sons, James, grew up to take on the trade of boot and shoe maker. In August 1845, at the age of 21, James married Rebecca Oliver in Dagenham Parish Church, and the following year their first child Alfred George Palmer was born. From the 1850s onwards James was connected with the parish church in various capacities, and in the mid-1860s he was elected parish clerk. In the autumn of 1878 he was appointed sexton, the official in charge of maintaining the fabric of the building. By now James Palmer was 54 years of age. He and Rebecca had produced at least twelve children, the youngest being Ruth, named after James's own mother. The couple and the younger members of their brood lived in Crown Street very close to the *Rose and Crown* pub, of which their eldest son Alfred was landlord.

One of the duties of Palmer's new post of sexton was that of grave digging, a task he had not done before. On Friday, 15 November 1878 Palmer entered the parish churchyard and began work on a new grave, the fifth or sixth he had dug since being appointed. The weather was very wet, making the job extremely difficult. Palmer eventually left off and resumed the following morning, but the rain did not cease.

At about 1 p.m. on the Saturday, Rebecca Palmer sent her youngest daughter, 10 year old Ruth, to the churchyard to tell her father that dinner was ready. The child went to the spot where he had been working, but to her dismay she found that the grave was full of earth. There was no sign of her father, although she could hear someone groaning. Ruth ran in fright across the road to the vicarage in Church Street, where one of her brothers worked as coachman to the vicar, Dr John Stevenson Moore. On hearing her story, the vicar and a band of helpers ran to the scene and began frantically digging. It took them half an hour to reach Palmer, however, by which time he was lifeless. He was eight feet below the ground, buried under at least a ton of earth.

At noon on Monday, two days after the tragedy, an inquest was held at the *Bull Inn*, Bull Street, before Charles Carne Lewis. Edmund Gill, a baker and corn dealer of Church Street, was elected foreman of the jury. They were told that there was a recently dug grave immediately next to the one Palmer was working on, and he had been throwing earth on top of it. The strip of solid earth between the two graves was little more than a foot wide. The continuous rain that had recently fallen must have softened and weakened it, so that eventually it became dislodged and

James Palmer's grave in a quiet corner of Dagenham Parish Churchyard. The Old Vicarage can be seen in the background. Authors' collection

caved in on top of Palmer. The coroner said it was 'a very injudicious thing to dig a grave eight feet deep in such weather and in such a manner.' The jury returned a verdict of 'Accidentally killed by the falling in of earth of a grave deceased was digging'.

James Palmer was buried on 23 November, and on the following day Dagenham's vicar, Dr Moore, preached a special sermon in his memory. The community gathered to pay their respects to one who had served it for so long, and to contribute to a collection on behalf of Palmer's widow Rebecca and her children. She remained in Dagenham, and three years later, at the time of the 1881 census, she was living in Church Street close to her son Alfred's pub, the *Rose & Crown*, and supporting herself as a dressmaker.

Sources

The Times
The *Essex Times*

Chapter 11

The Sinking of the *Princess Alice*, 1878

The scene was appalling. Hundreds of desperate men, women and children were fighting for their lives.

The hamlet of Creekmouth is situated where the River Roding flows into the Thames, two miles south of Barking. Here, in the late 1850s, Sir John Bennett Lawes built a chemical fertilizer factory together with two rows of workers' cottages. Creekmouth children experienced a village atmosphere in this isolated spot, but could also see the world's shipping pass by as it headed towards London's docks.

A modern view of the Thames from Creekmouth, looking towards the site of the Princess Alice disaster. The River Roding is on the right. The plaque in the foreground was designed by local schoolchildren. Authors' collection

It was Tuesday, 3 September 1878, and an air of excitement prevailed in Creekmouth. It was the long-awaited Treat Day for the youngsters. By mid-afternoon about 100 children had gathered in the meadow. Some were playing on swings that had been hired especially for the occasion. Others competed in running and jumping competitions, the winners being rewarded with shiny new pennies. At 5.30 p.m. it was tea-time, and the youngsters eagerly trooped into the homely flower-bedecked schoolroom, which had formerly been two cottages now knocked into one. They made short work of a delicious spread of bread, jam and cake, before dashing back outside for a few final rides on the swings while it was still light. The bell was then rung to call them back inside, where indoor games and yet more good things to eat awaited them. As 8 p.m. approached, the children were still full of energy, tearing about the schoolroom in their party hats and comical masks.

A short distance away, on the Thames, there was also a jolly atmosphere on board the pleasure steamer the *Princess Alice*. The 750 or so passengers were returning from an excursion to Gravesend, and some had joined in the impromptu singing as the vessel floated upriver past Creekmouth. Dusk had fallen but it was not yet completely dark. Shortly afterwards, at about 7.40 p.m., the ship reached Tripcock Point, opposite Beckton Gasworks. The people on deck heard a whistle blow, looked up and were horrified to see the immense bulk of an 890-ton collier, the *Bywell Castle*, bearing down on them. It ploughed into the starboard side of the *Princess Alice*, almost cutting her in two. She sank within minutes.

The crew of the *Bywell Castle* lowered ropes, anchor chains, ladders, boats and lifebuoys down to the water, and blew whistles to summon assistance. Boats and barges were rowed out from the shore in an attempt at rescue. The scene was appalling. Hundreds of desperate men, women and children were fighting for their lives. A barge skipper remembered that 'The whole river seemed alive with heads and hair. It looked like a river full of coconuts'.

To the inhabitants of Creekmouth, the collision had sounded like the boom of a big gun. Some ran to the river wall in time to see the light in the aft of the *Princess Alice* rise in the air and then disappear. For five minutes afterwards they heard screams and shrieks, and the moonlight revealed the terrible sight of the victims waving their arms about wildly as they battled to stay afloat. Back in the schoolroom, the children were about to start a game called kiss-in-the-ring when the supervisor was told of the collision. The party was abruptly brought to an end, and the children were given sweets and told to go home.

Meanwhile, a Lawes' factory manager gave orders for five boats to go to the scene and bring back as many survivors as possible. The schoolroom was chosen as the venue for their reception, and hastily-improvised beds made up. Soon the room, the scene of cheerful children's games just minutes before, looked like a hospital ward. Eighteen soaked, exhausted and injured people were brought in. The scene was heartrending. Most had been separated from their friends and relatives, including one man 'frantically lamenting over his wife and children, gone forever'. Schoolmaster Charles Minter and a team of helpers nursed them throughout the night. In a side passage was a young man who explained he had only managed to save himself by hanging onto the rigging. In a back room a table had been laid out for a celebration supper for the Treat Day helpers, and this was distributed among the survivors.

Other people plucked from the river were lodged at the nearby *Crooked Billet* pub, and around twenty more were taken into the workers' cottages. The Creekmouth curate wrote to the *Essex Times* praising the caring and unselfish reaction of the local people. They had taken survivors into their homes and watched at their bedsides all night, although they had to start work at 6 a.m. the following day:

> *The men are engaged in the hard work of Lawes' Chemical Manure Manufactury; but to see the way these rough-looking men set to work to save the drowning people did one's heart good, and I myself saw horny-handed men with hearts soft as women's gently bearing poor shipwrecked men and women in their arms, and bending over them bathing their wounds, soothing their mental agonies as they best knew how.*

The Creekmouth residents, he wrote, did not hesitate to donate their own shirts, trousers and waistcoats to the victims. 'Nothing was withheld that could in any way serve the poor sufferers. Best rooms, best beds were vacated, that the injured might have some little comfort.'

They were the lucky ones. Just over 100 people are known to have survived, most having been taken to Woolwich, on the southern shore of the Thames just upriver from Creekmouth. Several factors contributed to the low survival rate. The ship sank so quickly that hundreds were trapped inside, unable to reach the exits, and there was no time to lower lifeboats. Women were less likely than men to have learned to swim, and were hampered by their heavy skirts. By an unlucky chance the collision had occurred where the Northern Outfall sewer discharged its waste into the

Thames. Even strong swimmers had trouble staying afloat amidst the heavy, choking effluent. The scenes in the water were chaotic, as people fought each other to get onto the ropes and chains being dangled from the *Bywell Castle*. Others clung desperately to their neighbours, pulling them under to their deaths.

Soon dead bodies, rather than living survivors, were being brought to Creekmouth by the tireless bargemen. They were taken to the plumbers' room of the Lawes factory, and the following morning almost thirty corpses, chiefly those of women, were laid on sacks alongside each other awaiting identification. As the day wore on crowds of anxious people poured into Creekmouth seeking news of missing relatives and friends. They clustered round the list of survivors that had been posted on the schoolroom door, and then joined the queue outside Lawes to view the bodies. The *Essex Times* reporter noted that 'many a tearful eye turned from the awful scene, especially as they turned their gaze on the three children, who lay on a bench just below a window in the full light of day...who, contrary to the shocking aspect exhibited by the other bodies, lay side by side, as if sleeping'. There were also knots of people at the riverbank, gazing at the fatal scene. A small boat with a flag marked the spot where the tragic *Princess Alice* lay, and at low water the masts were visible.

Two days after the sinking, the coroner Charles C. Lewis arrived at Creekmouth to open the inquest on the bodies washed up on the Essex shore. Some had been found further downstream, at Dagenham and Rainham. The proceedings took place in the little schoolroom where some of the survivors had been cared for. The coroner's first task was to hear evidence of identification, and the inquest had to be adjourned and re-opened several times until this was complete. The state of many of the bodies made identification very difficult. One corpse had been identified by a relative, and a name ticket duly attached, but on arriving home the relative found the 'victim' alive and well, waiting for him. The last of the Creekmouth bodies to be positively identified was that of George Davis, a manager of Taylor & Walker's Brewery at Limehouse.

The coroner gave the order to release the bodies, and the *Essex Times* described the scene that followed:

> *For some distance in front of Messrs Lawes factory the road was lined with carts, traps, hearses and vehicles of all descriptions, each containing either a shell or a coffin for the reception of the bodies, and as one after another was*

brought out there was scarcely a dry eye along the immense concourse of persons, especially when the coffins of the poor little children came into view.

Those who still remained anonymous were sent for burial in a communal grave at Woolwich Cemetery.

Four members of one family killed in the disaster were laid to rest at St Margaret's Church in Barking. They were 34 year old brewery worker George Michael Huddle, his wife Eliza, aged 31, and their sons Ernest Leopold aged 3 and 7 week old Henry Francis. The family lived at Bethnal Green but George's father, Thomas Huddle, was originally from Barking, which is presumably the reason they were buried there. The epitaph reads:

They were taken all together,
In death they now lie side by side.
Such was God's will: we dare not ask
The reason why. Reader, be ready.

Finally, is it known why the collision occurred? A tragic misunderstanding seems to be to blame. By convention, pleasure steamers going upriver stayed close to the southern shoreline as they rounded Tripcock Point. Although William Grinstead, captain of the *Princess Alice*, drowned in the disaster, it is probable that this was the route he was taking. Thus the steamer's port side was close to the shore. There was a little known (and not legally binding) rule that when steam vessels met on the river they should pass port to port. This would have meant the *Princess Alice* moving out into midstream and letting the *Bywell Castle* pass on the southern shore side.

As Creekmouth people were well aware, there were strong currents in that part of the Thames. It seems that just as the *Princess Alice* reached Tripcock Point she was drawn by one of these currents towards the centre of the river. The *Bywell Castle* captain assumed that the steamer had pulled out in order to pass him port to port. The *Princess Alice*, however, went back towards the southern shore, and the *Bywell Castle* hit her on the starboard side just in front of the central paddle box.

Even if one accepts that the disaster was the result of a misunderstanding, Captain Grinstead had made a decision earlier in the evening that may well have contributed towards the tragedy. The helmsman wanted to stay behind at Gravesend as it was his night off, and asked a friend, John Eyres, who happened to be on board as a passenger, to stand in for him on the return journey. Captain Grinstead agreed to the

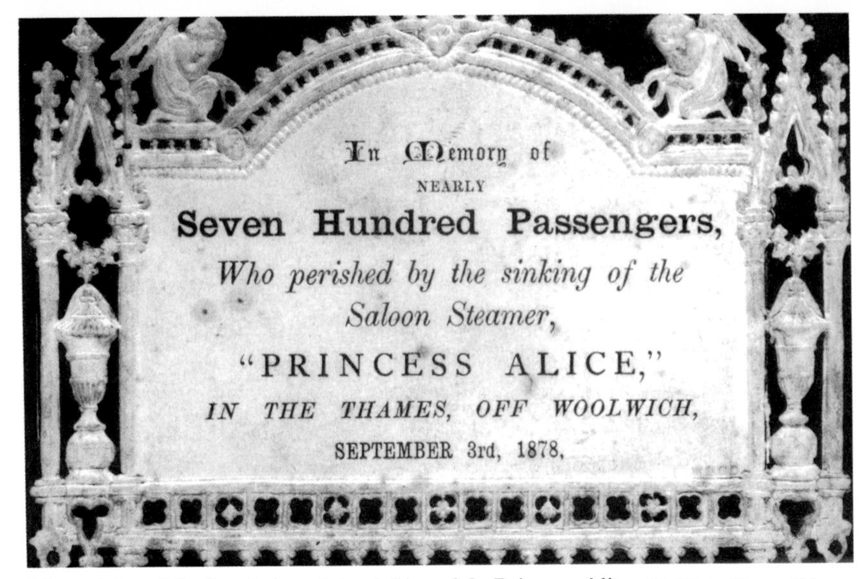

Memorial card for the victims of the sinking of the Princess Alice. LBBD Archives at Valence House Museum

substitution. Eyres was an Able Seaman but had little experience of piloting vessels along the Thames, and had never steered a vessel as long as the *Princess Alice*. It seems unbelievable to modern eyes that the highly skilled task was given to an unqualified person. Eyres, ironically, was to survive the sinking.

Princess Alice, after whom the ill-fated steamer was named, was a daughter of Queen Victoria. The year 1878 also brought tragedy to her own family in the form of diphtheria. On 16 November her youngest daughter died of the disease and, on 14 December, Princess Alice herself followed, aged just 35.

The sinking still remains the worst-ever disaster on a British waterway. Strangely, the *Bywell Castle* was also to end her days in a tragic fashion. She disappeared in the Bay of Biscay five and a half years later, and neither she nor her crew were ever seen again.

Sources

The Times
The *Essex Times*
Guest, Edwin: *The Wreck of the Princess Alice* (1878)
Thurston, Gavin: *The Great Thames Disaster* (1965)
Neal, Wendy: *With disastrous consequences* (1992)
Withington, John: *Capital disasters* (2003)

Chapter 12

By Their Own Hand

You've been attempting to destroy yourselves.
Why not tell me all about it?

John McAllister, 1868

Ten years before the tragic sinking of the *Princess Alice* off Creekmouth, the residents of the tiny Thameside hamlet were welcoming in the New Year of 1868. Among the employees of the Lawes manure factory were the McAllister brothers from Glasgow. The eldest, John, aged 39, was a manager, and Robert and Alexander worked as plumbers. They and their families dwelt in the terraced houses built by Lawes for its employees close to their place of work.

His neighbours may have been exchanging festive greetings and renditions of *Auld Lang Syne*, but John McAllister could see no reason to be cheerful. The previous month, the Irish republican group, the Fenian Brotherhood, had planted a bomb at Clerkenwell Prison, killing several Londoners. John had displayed a depressed and anxious mood for some time, and now became obsessed by the threat posed by the Fenians. He also had fears, probably groundless, that he was about to lose his job. Added to this, it was apparent to all around him that he had a drink problem.

Throughout that winter, Mary McAllister had frequently called Dr Frederick Davidson of East Street, Barking to see her husband. On the evening of Monday, 6 January the medical man travelled yet again in his pony and trap down the rough track leading from Barking Town to Creekmouth. When Davidson arrived at 6, Factory Cottages, where the McAllisters lived with their children, he found John 'low and nervous'. Robert McAllister also called to see his brother that evening, and John told him 'he thought he should not live long, but he did not know why, except that he complained of pains in his heart and head'. John also forced Robert to listen to a tirade of complaints, presumably unfounded, about his wife Mary.

The following day Robert called again, and found John still fretting

Creekmouth Cottages. Barking Power Station, seen in the background, was opened in 1925. LBBD Archives at Valence House Museum

about the Fenian attacks: 'Those Fenians are about, and I am sure something mysterious will happen before morning...they are picking out all the leading men'. He begged Robert not to go home. To appease him, Robert said 'give me your revolver and I will stop outside all night'. Their brother Alexander also called that evening. John seemed to him to be 'dull in spirits' and had 'appeared strange in his manner and conversation, often asking the same question three or four times over'.

At that time John and Mary McAllister had 11 year old Maud Maria Fear staying with them. At about 9 a.m. the following day, Wednesday, 8 January, Maud and the McAllisters were having breakfast in the kitchen. John finished his meal and asked his wife to pour his cup of tea while he went upstairs to wash. About ten minutes later Mary McAllister and her young visitor were suddenly startled by the sound of a gunshot from the upper floor. Mrs McAllister immediately ran upstairs. Little Maud heard her ask frantically 'Where *are* you?' but there was no reply from John.

After a few moments' silence the house rang with Mrs McAllister's voice shrieking 'He's dead! Murder! Murder!' Robert McAllister, who lived two doors away, heard the noise and rushed into the house. He met Mary in the kitchen, and she cried out 'Robert, Robert, he has killed himself!'

The shocking scene that met Robert's eyes upstairs confirmed that his brother had indeed ended his own life. John was lying face down with his right arm underneath him. Between his legs there was a double-barrelled breech-loader gun. John had committed suicide in the most determined fashion. He had tied a piece of bell rope to each of the two triggers of the gun, then attached the ends of the rope to one of his feet. Finally, he had stood up and pulled the muzzle of the gun towards his head, thus setting off the triggers. His brains were spattered across the ceiling and furniture of the room.

Dr Davidson was called, and he and John's brothers turned the body over. They found that only the right hand barrel of the gun had actually discharged, but it was enough to have caused instant death. The front part of John McAllister's face had been totally blown away by the force of the blast.

Two days later Charles Carne Lewis arrived at the *Crooked Billet* at Creekmouth to preside over the inquest. Having steeled themselves for the gruesome task of viewing poor John McAllister's body, the coroner and jury heard Robert explain that his brother had first suffered from mental illness sixteen or eighteen years previously, when he had been 'a little deranged'. Frederick Davidson was also called, and declared that although the dead man was clearly not in his right mind, he had 'never appeared to me to be suicidal'. The jury, after a short consultation, returned a verdict of 'Temporary Insanity'.

John McAllister's funeral took place at St Margaret's Church in Barking on 14 January. The cortège was followed by fourteen of his friends and relations as well as about twenty of the workmen from Lawes, all wearing bands of black crape around their hats. Virtually all the shopkeepers in Barking closed their shutters in a gesture of respect. A huge crowd, estimated at over 400, gathered in the churchyard as the Reverend Henry Seymour presided over the burial. This demonstration of support, together with a report in the *Essex Times* declaring that 'Mr McAllister was highly respected by everyone', contradicts the popular view that the Victorians were unsympathetic towards people who committed suicide.

Arthur Duffield, 1887

It was March 1887, and Britain was preparing to celebrate Queen Victoria's Golden Jubilee. William Duffield, a baker and confectioner of 17 The Broadway, Barking, was no doubt planning to stock his shop with a delicious array of cakes and sweets to mark the great occasion. Mr Duffield's 21 year old son Arthur, however, had his mind fixed on a lady boasting more obvious charms than those of the elderly monarch. About three months previously Arthur had made the acquaintance of Emma Amelia Allen, known as Millie, who was six years his senior. She worked as a dressmaker for a Mr Martin who had a business making and retailing ladies' mantles (fashionable shoulder capes) in Burnt Ash Road, Lee, near Blackheath. As was usual at that time, Miss Allen and other employees lived above the premises. When Arthur Duffield met the young lady he was instantly smitten, and soon afterwards made her a proposal of marriage, which she accepted.

On Monday, 28 March Arthur had tea at about 6 p.m. with his parents, brothers and sisters. He had always been a rather quiet and reserved lad, and although his family knew of his relationship with Miss Allen he had not told his parents about their engagement. He had, however, confided in his elder brother Harry, who also had a business as a baker elsewhere in Barking. After the meal Arthur went to Barking Station and bought a return ticket to Lee Station via Fenchurch Street. The stationmaster, Mr Masters, was to recall that Arthur chatted with him about the weather in the normal way. He left Barking by the 6.40 p.m. train and arrived at Mr Martin's shop, the home of Millie Allen, about an hour and a half later.

Barking Station, photographed around 1906. Arthur Duffield took his last journey from here. LBBD Archives at Valence House Museum

Walter John Hucksteph, the porter, was putting up the shutters when Arthur Duffield approached and slipped twopence into his hand. Would he do him the favour of telling Miss Allen that someone wanted to see her? The message was duly given. Millie was taken by surprise, and said at first 'Oh, I can't go out tonight'. She then went to the shop door and spoke to her fiancé. He greeted her with a kiss and managed to persuade her to change her mind about coming out. The young lady returned briefly to put on her hat and outer clothes, then the pair stepped out into the evening darkness.

According to Miss Allen, Arthur suggested they turn off the main road and into a field. She was unwilling to take that route, but he gripped her arm and dragged her behind him. After a while he suddenly turned on her, pushed her to the ground and cried 'Millie, you must die!' She blacked out for a short time, and on recovering consciousness saw him running away. She managed to get to her feet and stagger out of the field and back to Mr Martin's shop. The housemaid Martha Desbrey was working in the kitchen when she was startled by the sight of Millie standing at the door. She was hatless, and her hair, usually carefully pinned up, was hanging down and disordered. Most dreadful of all was the sight of streams of blood pouring from her face and neck. A local medical man, Dr Williams, was called. He examined the stricken young lady and found she had a terrible gash in her throat from under the ear to her chin, and stab wounds at the back of her neck.

Two police officers, Inspector Broadbridge and Sergeant Newton, soon arrived and went to the field in which Millie had been attacked. The beam of light from their lamp revealed a human shape lying on the ground. It proved to be the dead body of Arthur Duffield. He had cut his own throat so deeply that his head was almost severed from his body. An open razor was found sticking into the ground close by. Millie Allen was immediately taken to Guy's Hospital, where it was announced that, in spite of the terrible appearance of her injuries, her life was not in serious danger.

The inquest into the death of Arthur Duffield opened the following day at the *Northbrook Hotel*, in Burnt Ash Road. Until this point, the sympathies of all had been with Miss Allen. Harry Duffield, though, stated to the coroner and jury that the relationship had caused his brother nothing but stress and heartache. He portrayed Millie Allen as a scheming money-grabber who, since their engagement, had insisted on taking most of Arthur's wages to pass on to her unemployed father. She had challenged her fiancé to give her up, declaring that if he did she would sue him for breach of promise of marriage – a criminal offence at that time. Harry Duffield said that Millie and Arthur had recently visited him, and he had noticed that she treated his brother in a very offhand manner. The worry of it all had caused Arthur to have serious difficulty sleeping, which had only served to make him even more anxious and depressed.

According to Harry, Arthur had shown him a letter he intended to send to Miss Allen in the hope that she would choose to break off the engagement herself in writing, thus protecting him from the charge of breach of promise. Harry explained that among a batch of letters discovered in Arthur's bedroom there was one which read: 'My dear Millie – seeing it is time this farce was brought to a conclusion, I ask if you want to give me up or not. I am willing either way, but the answer must be written in ink, and sent to me, or I will not take your answer'. There was also a torn-off fragment of another anguished letter: 'My dearest Millie. – On my bended knees I humbly beseech you [...] writing to you I cannot express my sorrow. Believe me when I say the grief which lies in my breast is killing me by degrees. Do believe me, your promised husband. I solemnly promise that my neglect shall not [...]'

Another was one Arthur had received from Millie. It was dated 9 March, and she had written: 'Dear Arthur, will you please be here tomorrow evening (Thursday) at 8 o'clock? Your strange note, also your indifferent manner to me on Saturday evening last demands an explanation. My answer to your question you will find fully decisive...'

Faced with such baffling missives, the coroner decided it was essential for them to hear from Millie Allen herself. He therefore adjourned the inquest to allow time for her to recover sufficiently to be able to appear, and it was not until Monday, 2 May, nearly five weeks later, that the proceedings were resumed. The throng of press and public turned expectantly towards Miss Allen as she stepped forward to give her evidence. She was dressed in black, and journalists noted that she was of medium height and had a dark complexion. She seemed bodily very weak, and spoke in a low tone.

Millie stated that the attack had happened so quickly she hadn't even noticed the razor in Arthur's hand. She told the coroner that her fiancé wasn't particularly affectionate towards her, and was inclined to jealousy. She denied having asked for or received any money from him, although he had occasionally given her presents as would have been expected. She was shown the letter in which Arthur had written 'it is time this farce was brought to a conclusion', but said he never sent it or anything like it. She emphasized that she had never had a letter from him asking her to give up the engagement, that it was never broken off, and that he didn't raise the subject on the evening of the attack.

William Duffield, Arthur's father, said his son 'was of very temperate habits' so there was no question of his mind having been affected by alcohol or drugs. When asked further about his son's health, he explained that Arthur had suffered from severe heat stroke during a voyage from Australia several years before. As the ship was coming through the Red Sea Arthur had fainted away on deck.

At the conclusion of the evidence, the jury returned a verdict that Arthur died 'by cutting his throat whilst labouring under temporary mental derangement'. But what drove him to such extreme measures – attempted murder and suicide – remains a mystery.

Arthur Hill and Emily Spooner, 1894

In the summer of 1894 Emily Spooner, aged 21, was working as a mother's help at a house in Clifton Terrace, Southend. About eighteen months previously she had met 22 year old Arthur Rowland Harrington Hill, a solicitor's clerk who was studying hard to qualify as a lawyer. The pair fell in love, and in time became engaged to be married. This was, however, against the wishes of Emily's parents, who lived at Heath Farm in Orsett, Essex. Arthur Hill's father, now dead, had been a doctor. The young man now resided with his mother, brothers and sisters at Ecclesbourne, a house in Clements Road, Ilford.

Towards the end of August Emily received a letter from her fiancé. He wrote that his exam results had come through – and he had failed. He was also worried because he had pawned a watch belonging to his late father, and couldn't afford to redeem it. He could see no way out of his troubles apart from ending his own life. Arthur wanted to meet Emily as soon as possible, so she was waiting when he stepped off a train at Southend on the evening of Saturday, 25 August. His resolve was not to be shaken. Suicide, he told her, was his only option, and he would carry it out that very night. Emily said that if that was the case then she would die with him.

At about 8 p.m. the pair took a train from Southend to Dagenham station (now called Dagenham East). They walked through Dagenham

An early photograph of Church Elm Lane. In a field near this spot, Arthur and Emily planned to carry out their suicide pact. LBBD Archives at Valence House Museum

Village, and sat down in an isolated field off Church Elm Lane. Arthur wrote a short note of farewell: 'Dear Ma, I enclose pawn ticket with regret that I die cheating my mother. Please pay Mr Bodlie 10s that I owe him. It is not right that he should suffer, and he needs the money'.

Arthur then produced two bottles of laudanum, which they drank. Altogether there were eight pennyworths of the liquid, and although it soon put them both into a stupor it was nowhere near enough to be fatal. Emily was doubled up with stomach pains, and, knowing that Arthur was carrying a small table knife, begged him to 'stab me or kill me somehow'. He then stabbed her in the neck. It proved to be merely a surface wound, so he struck her again, this time in the chest, but the knife entered just under the heart. Still she remained conscious, so he stabbed her in the arm, and then cut his own throat. But having failed to kill Emily, he was dismayed to find that he too was still alive, although both had lost a lot of blood.

The pair then got up and staggered away, weak and confused. For nearly twenty-four hours they wandered aimlessly through the fields of

Dagenham. They had had nothing to eat at all. At one point they accidentally fell into a brook, the water having been screened from view by reeds, and their clothes were covered in filthy slime. On Sunday evening the dazed couple stumbled into the yard of Mardyke Farm in Rainham. The farmer, William Curtis, noticed that the girl's eyes were bloodshot and prominent, her hair was down her back, and she had a wound near her left collarbone. He saw a similar slash across the young man's throat. Curtis offered to help them, and Hill asked for some water for them to wash with. Emily tried to explain away their strange appearance by declaring that they had been set upon by a gang of roughs, but the farmer saw through the pretence immediately. 'You've been attempting to destroy yourselves. Why not tell me all about it?' Hill then admitted the truth, saying that there had not been enough laudanum to kill them, so 'We then used a knife, but it was too horrible'.

Curtis asked the pair to promise they would not do it again, and Hill said they were in a different frame of mind now and just wanted to go home. He asked for a hat for Emily, who had lost hers, and also a neckerchief for himself. The farmer gave them the items, then watched the couple take their leave at about 6 p.m. They still loitered about, though, so he reported the matter to the police. Arthur and Emily eventually made their way to Chadwell Heath railway station, reaching there at about 10 p.m. He travelled to his home in Ilford, and she bought a ticket to nearby Romford where she had a married sister living in Waterloo Road.

Back at Southend, Emily's disappearance the previous day had caused the alarm to be raised. Her parents Thomas and Eliza were naturally extremely worried, and on Monday morning they travelled to Romford to tell their other daughter what had happened. To their astonishment they found Emily had arrived there overnight, dazed and with blood-soaked clothes. She had refused to tell her sister what had happened to her. Dr McKenzie was called, and after examining the young lady he pronounced that her life was not in danger in spite of the great loss of blood. He said that the wound under her heart was the most serious one, but that luckily her ribs had protected her.

During that day a letter arrived for her. It read:

My darling Emilie, I do hope you are safe…If this should prove my ruin, forgive and forget me. Whatever happens, I shall always love and remember

> *you. I can hardly forgive myself for leaving you at Chadwell Heath station, but I was so done up. Emily, I love you more than ever. Please write and say that you do not entirely hate me as I deserve. Arthur.*

Emily was persuaded to tell the police the whole sad story, and later that day Arthur Hill was arrested at his Ilford home. As he was being taken away to the local police station, his astounded neighbours noticed that a large bandage around his neck prevented him from wearing a collar and tie. Hill was brought before the Stratford magistrates charged with the attempted murder of Emily Spooner and also with attempting to commit suicide (incidentally, a criminal offence until 1961). He was described as 'a fine strapping fellow...tall, dark-haired...with peculiar-looking eyes, and a blackish moustache'.

Emily was summoned to give evidence against him, and on Saturday, 1 September she was called into the witness box. The press and public saw 'a lady of below the medium height, and evidently of a quiet disposition. She was very pale, and had some blotches on her face, while her bloodshot eyes gave her countenance a strange appearance. She wore a veil'. No sooner had Emily mounted the steps, however, than she fainted and had to be taken away. When she had recovered she told her story clearly. She had to repeat her evidence at a later hearing, at which point her health had obviously improved, for she was then described as 'decidedly pretty, neatly dressed in black, but...very pale and delicate'. Arthur Hill was remanded in custody until his trial at the next Essex Assizes.

Two months later Hill was brought into the dock at the Shire Hall in Chelmsford. He was described as 'a smart and well-dressed young fellow, and who, since his imprisonment, has grown a beard and whiskers'. The Grand Jury rejected the indictment of attempted murder. At first Hill pleaded not guilty to the charge of attempted suicide, but afterwards withdrew the plea and confessed his guilt. The judge, Mr Baron Pollock, told him: 'It is a wretched thing to see a person who has got the power of body and education that you have, falling into such miserable, selfish, false conception of your duty to yourself and all mankind that led you to commit an offence of this kind'. He sentenced Hill to a month's hard labour for the attempted suicide.

Meanwhile, Emily worked as a tobacconist's assistant at Tottenham until 8 May 1895, when she returned home to Orsett. When Arthur was set free from prison he was given permission to renew contact with her. On 10 June she received a telegram from him, reading: 'Holiday. Shall be at Grays at eleven o'clock. Arthur'. Emily headed towards Grays Station only to find him walking down the road towards her, having arrived early. It took little persuasion for her to return to the station with him and take the next train to London. They had lunch at Fenchurch Street, then travelled to King's Cross and from thence to Welwyn in Hertfordshire, arriving at about 5 p.m. They walked for a while until they reached a place called Sandy Bottom. Darkness was falling and Emily said it must be time to go home. Arthur's reply was: 'We are not going home tonight. I have no money, we can't go back'. They then sat down by the roadside. Emily asked what he was going to do, and he declared 'I intend to kill you and then myself!'

Arthur took a razor from his pocket, opened it and drew it across her throat, inflicting a wound on the left side of her neck three inches long and half an inch deep. This time Emily refused to cooperate. She fought back, desperately trying to grab the razor, but fainted in the attempt. When she came round she saw Hill sitting by her side with blood pouring from his own throat. Yet again, however, his attempt at killing had failed, for he was still very much alive. Emily murmured 'What did you do it for?' and he replied he did not know. They remained at the spot all night, and in the morning Arthur fetched some milk and bandaged her neck with a handkerchief. They walked some way towards Hatfield, then Hill asked her to wait while he sold his watch to raise money to get back to London.

Emily waited three-quarters of an hour before deciding to walk on. When Inspector Boutell of the Hertfordshire Police spotted her bloodstained figure staggering along the Welwyn Road, he immediately had her taken to the police station. She was examined by Cuthbert Dale, a surgeon, who announced that happily her life was not in danger. The scar of her old wound was still visible close to the new one.

It turned out that Arthur was, at that time, also in custody under the same roof. He had approached a man and asked if he wanted to buy a Waterbury watch for four shillings, not realizing that he was talking to a plain-clothes policeman named Sergeant G. Reed. Noticing blood on Hill's throat, collar and waistcoat, Reed asked him to account for it, and was not satisfied with the explanation that it was the result of a boil on his neck.

At the end of June Arthur Hill was again in the dock, this time at the Hertford Assizes. He pleaded guilty on two counts – attempting to murder Emily Spooner and attempting to commit suicide. He was sentenced to eighteen months' hard labour on the first charge, to be followed by six months' hard labour on the second. We do not know whether the couple met again after his release. There is certainly no record of them marrying. Let us hope that after her two close brushes with death, Emily's subsequent life was a happy and uneventful one.

Sources

The Times
The *Essex Times*
The *Essex County Standard*

Chapter 13

The Infant Witness: Martha Bodger 1887

There was blood everywhere – across her throat, on the floor, and across the walls.

Anyone travelling southwards along the Romford Road from Chigwell Row towards Hog Hill in 1887, the year of Queen Victoria's Golden Jubilee, would have seen a row of four terraced houses, known as Beale's Cottages, come into view on the right-hand side. The tenant of the second cottage was 27 year old James Bodger, a gardener working for Mr Frank Green, a ship owner and Justice of the Peace living

Hog Hill, from an old postcard. LBBD Archives at Valence House Museum

at nearby Hainault Lodge. Bodger was known as a conscientious and hard worker, and he began Tuesday, 11 October 1887 in his usual energetic way, rising at 4 a.m. and spending the next hour and a half whitewashing a room. He then lit the kitchen fire and put the kettle on to boil.

At about 5.40 a.m. James took a cup of tea up to his 24 year old wife Martha in the front bedroom. On his way up the stairs he passed their lodger, Joseph Morley, a 17 year old journeyman blacksmith from Newton in Suffolk. James greeted his wife with a cheery 'Good morning', and they kissed affectionately. Martha told him she would get up soon and clean the room he had whitewashed, and as he turned to leave she asked 'You will be home for dinner?' The couple had met when Martha, whose maiden name was Smith, was a servant at a nearby house in Chigwell, and had married in February 1884 in Martha's home village of Steeple Ashton in Wiltshire. They had a 6 month old baby girl, Amy Elizabeth, who lay in the bed beside her mother.

Bodger closed the bedroom door behind him and went downstairs. He entered the kitchen, and he and Joseph Morley made some breakfast to take to work with them. Morley, a short and stocky youth with quiet manners, had been with the Bodgers since the beginning of the year, only vacating his room for a short period at the time of baby Amy's birth in March. Bodger left the house at about 5.45, reminding his lodger to pull the front door after him when he came out.

A couple named Emma and William Mansfield lived next door with their children. Emma Mansfield was lying in bed at about 5.50 that morning when she heard screaming coming through the thin wall separating her bedroom from that of Martha Bodger. The noise lasted about a minute and was 'like anybody in hysterics'. Mrs Mansfield opened her window and looked out. The Bodgers' neighbour on the other side, Thomas Briant, had come into his front garden, having also heard the noise. With him was his niece Maria Day. Briant had, at first, thought the screams were caused by boys playing in the road, but saw that there was no one about. Emma Mansfield called over to him from her window, saying she couldn't think what was the matter.

Briant then tried the Bodgers' front door, but found it locked. He decided that perhaps Martha Bodger's baby had fallen out of bed causing her to panic, and went back to own cottage to finish his breakfast. His niece was already back inside, and told him she'd heard a man's heavy

Hainault Lodge, where James Bodger worked as a gardener. LBBD Archives at Valence House Museum

footsteps coming from the floorboards of the Bodgers' back kitchen. Thomas Briant felt decidedly uneasy. He worked with James Bodger at Hainault Lodge, on Hog Hill, and decided to go there immediately and tell his neighbour something might be wrong at home.

While Briant prepared to leave, his niece Maria heard the Bodgers' front door close. She looked out, curious to know who had left the house, and saw the figure of Joseph Morley, wearing a dark jacket and hard hat.

He sauntered off towards his place of work, Mr Frank Messent's blacksmith's shop at the junction of Romford Road and the New North Road, just over 200 yards away. Maria was not the only person to see Morley leave that morning. A teenage boy named Henry Simon Barton was on his way to work at nearby Foxburrows Farm when he stopped as usual at Beale's Cottages to pick up a workmate, one of Emma Mansfield's sons. Henry yelled 'Frank, are you ready?' but it was four or five minutes before his companion appeared. While waiting, the lad saw Morley emerge from the front door of Bodger's cottage. Henry knew Morley, and called out 'Hallo Joe', but got no answer.

Meanwhile, James Bodger had reached his place of work, and was stoking a fire in a greenhouse when Thomas Briant approached. On hearing what he had to say, Bodger lost no time in returning home. Alone, he entered his house by the back door and went upstairs to the landing. His bedroom door was open, and a terrible sight met his eyes. Martha was lying on her back across the centre of the bed. Her nightdress was pulled up towards her waist, leaving her lower body exposed. Her legs hung over the side of the bed facing the door, the feet not quite touching the ground. There was blood everywhere – across her throat, on the floor, and across the walls. The blanket, counterpane and sheet lay on the floor, and were also saturated with blood.

Bodger didn't enter the room, but immediately ran back downstairs and pulled open the front door where an anxious knot of neighbours waited. 'Martha has been murdered!' he cried. 'Never!' they exclaimed, and someone asked whether the baby was dead too. In the shock of the moment, James had not even thought about little Amy. He somehow found the courage to go back up and face the shocking scene once more. The baby was covered in blood but quite unhurt, lying close by the head of her dead mother. She showed delight at seeing her father. 'The child was alive and laughing at me', he sorrowfully recalled. Bodger picked up his daughter, took her downstairs and handed her to one of his neighbours.

Joseph Morley, meanwhile, had arrived at Frank Messent's forge on the New North Road at 6.30, half an hour later than usual. He was hard at work when James Bodger suddenly burst in, grabbed him by the wrist and shouted 'Frank, this man has been and killed my wife!' Messent replied 'No, never, Jim!' but Bodger insisted 'He has, he's killed her!' Morley calmly denied it, saying 'No I ain't, Jim'. Bodger was in no doubt. 'Yes you did!' he yelled, and turning to Messent he said 'Yes, Frank, it's true, you come and see'.

Just across the road from the forge was the *Old Hainault Oak* pub. Messent fetched the landlord, William Ernest Drake, and they accompanied Bodger and Morley the short distance to Beale's Cottages. Mrs Lydia Button, who lived next door to the forge, walked with them. She reached the cottage just before the others, and went up to the bedroom. Mrs Button first cried out 'Good God! She has broken a blood vessel!' but then noticed that Martha's throat had been cut so deeply that her head was nearly severed. Mrs Button pulled out a clean sheet and spread it over the body. Messent and Drake then had a brief look at the scene before returning to the forge. Morley ambled back with them, his hands in his pockets.

Amy Elizabeth Bodger at about two years old. As a baby she was present when her mother was murdered. Private collection

A neighbour had gone to Chigwell Row to fetch medical help, and at about 7.15 a.m. Dr George Jameson arrived at the house. Lydia Button went upstairs with him and pulled back the sheet. Martha's hands and feet were now cold, but there was still some warmth left in her body. Jameson found four distinct cuts across her throat, each at least seven inches long. He reported that 'Her throat was cut from an inch below the lobe of the left ear deeply in a slanting direction downwards to below the angle of the jaw on the opposite side…All the important large blood vessels on the left side of her neck were wounded some being completely cut across'. Martha also had a long gash along her cheek, from her mouth to the left ear, caused most probably by her knocking her attacker's arm aside. There were also two deep cuts on her left finger and thumb where, in desperation, she must have clutched the blade of the murder weapon. The doctor glanced down and noticed the handle of a razor lying on the floor. No blade was visible. Despite Martha's nightdress being pulled back, Dr Jameson found no evidence of a sexual assault. Her dress and purse were hanging by the bed. No money had been taken.

On getting back to the forge, Frank Messent asked 'Joe, did you murder this woman?' The answer was a decided 'No', and Messent then said 'Joe, if you know anything about it, say so'. 'I don't', was the reply. Messent then went into the road and looked carefully at Morley, who was standing against the workshop door. He noticed a spot of blood, about the size of a two-shilling piece, on the left breast of Morley's coat. He said 'Joe, this looks rather bad for you'. Morley argued that he'd cut his finger falling off his bicycle the evening before, and repeated 'I didn't do it, Frank'. Morley then went to the lavatory, and had been inside for about three minutes when Dr Jameson arrived and called out to him. When Morley emerged, Jameson examined his clothing. He found further patches of blood on Morley's coat and the knees of his trousers. His shirt was also bloodstained, and it seemed that he had turned it inside out while in the lavatory in an attempt to hide the stains. When asked to account for the blood, Morley said 'I suppose it is from this', showing Jameson a triangular cut about 3/4 inch across on the forefinger of his right hand. Once again he blamed a fall from his bicycle.

Dr Jameson went back to Beale's Cottages to examine baby Amy, and found her unhurt although 'the clothes were saturated with blood'. She was put into the temporary care of Mrs Alice Green of Hainault Lodge, wife of James Bodger's employer. On the way to the cottage the doctor had kept his eyes to the ground, and at about twenty-four or twenty-five paces from the cottage he found a pool of blood, mixed with mucous and saliva, 'as if someone had been sucking a wound'.

Jameson then returned to the forge and told Morley to take his hands out of his pockets. There was blood under the fingernails of both hands. As well as the cut already shown to him on Morley's right hand, he saw another longer cut on the back of the third finger of the left hand. This wound, nearly two inches deep, went down to the bone. Jameson saw that though it had stopped bleeding it was still moist, so it must have been present only an hour or two at most. Messent and Drake kept a close eye on Morley until 9.20 a.m., when Sub-Inspector Thomas Saunders of Barkingside Police arrived and announced he was arresting him. Morley displayed a 'dreamy unconcerned manner' and replied 'Very well, I suppose I must go then'. He was handed over to a constable and escorted to Barkingside Police Station.

Inspector Saunders and Chief Inspector James Cudmore of Woodford Police then carried out a thorough search of Bodger's cottage. They saw that at one place on the bedroom floor there had been an attempt to wipe up the blood. Going into Morley's bedroom, they noticed three spots of fresh blood on the carpet and smears on the door-handle. There were further splashes all down the staircase, on the staircase door, in the back kitchen and around the sink in the scullery. The officers also found a patch of blood upon the downstairs window blind, showing that the killer must have been watching while Thomas Briant was trying to open the front door.

The policemen then departed, leaving Lydia Button to lay out the body and do her best to clear up the room. She turned over a strip of carpet by the bedside, and underneath she found the blade of the razor, covered in blood. The murderer had stabbed with such sheer force as to cause the blade to snap away from the handle.

The inquest opened at the *Old Hainault Oak* on Friday, 14 October. James Bodger told the coroner that the murder weapon was his own razor, which he used only on Sundays. He always put it out of harm's way on top of a cupboard in the kitchen, and Morley knew where it was kept. George Jameson reported that he had carried out a post-mortem that morning on Martha's body. As well as the vicious knife wounds, he found that she had suffered a heavy blow to the left side of her head. The funeral took place on Sunday, 16 October at Chigwell Row. A large crowd of sympathizers stood in silence as Martha's coffin was borne from her home to the churchyard on the shoulders of four men. James was so overcome at the graveside he had to be led away.

On Friday, 4 November Morley stood in the dock at the Shire Hall in Chelmsford, and pleaded not guilty to a charge of murder. He was described in the press as 'Below the medium height, and of entirely youthful appearance...a large head, a somewhat prominent forehead, intelligent eyes, a mouth with a very firm expression'. Morley's defence barrister argued that the case against him was entirely circumstantial (at that time there was no scientific means of identifying individual blood samples), and that he lacked a motive. The jury, however, returned a verdict of guilty as soon as the judge's summing-up ended, without even retiring from the room to confer. The dreadful sentence of death by hanging was then passed, and Morley heard it without showing the slightest concern.

Not long afterwards, Morley confessed his guilt to the Springfield Gaol chaplain, William Lumley. He said he was deeply sorry for what had happened, that he hadn't planned to kill Martha, but had yielded to an uncontrollable impulse. He claimed an obsession with reading about true-life murders and other crimes, and said he had been particularly drawn to a recent case in which the vicar of Cretingham in Suffolk had been killed by his own curate – his throat cut with a razor as he lay in bed. Morley denied attempted rape, although, as we have seen, he did pull up Martha's nightdress, and it was claimed that he had previously indecently assaulted a servant girl at the *Old Hainault Oak*.

An appeal against Morley's death sentence was sent to the Home Secretary, the main grounds being his extreme youth (only 17 years old) and the existence of insanity in his family. A report on his mental state was drawn up by Dr George Amsden from the Brentwood Lunatic Asylum and a surgeon from Broadmoor. They ruled that Morley was not insane, and the appeal was rejected. His execution was set for Monday, 21 November 1887.

The events came as a huge shock to Morley's home village of Newton in Suffolk. The blacksmith spoke of the 'quiet, well-behaved lad' who had worked in his smithy for two years. The village schoolmistress stated that he been a 'quiet, docile and obedient pupil', and his heartbroken mother said he was a general favourite, and that 'everyone liked him'. Morley's brothers travelled to Springfield to say their goodbyes. On entering the cell they found him sitting with his elbows on the little table, face buried in his hands. When they asked him why he had committed the crime, there was no answer, just a loud sobbing. The final and most poignant visit was on the day before the execution, when Morley's father Benjamin came to take a last farewell, accompanied by his youngest and favourite sister Mary Ann, known as Polly, whom he had particularly asked to see.

Morley awoke the following morning after a good night's sleep, and was given a breakfast of fish with bread and butter. The prison bell began to toll, and the executioner, 35 year old Yorkshireman and ex-policeman James Berry, willingly chatted to waiting press reporters. He told them that the youngest man he had hanged so far had been 19 years old, and that the rope he was about to use was five-eighths of an inch in diameter and had done duty once before, at Oxford the previous week. He said he intended to give Morley a long drop of seven feet, as he weighed barely eight stone. In this respect Berry was more humane than his predecessor William Calcraft, a practitioner of the strangling short drop.

At a few minutes before 8 a.m. Berry entered Morley's cell, and the prisoner submitted calmly to the pinioning of his arms. When the time came to leave, Morley was groaning heavily and had to be supported by two warders. Executions were no longer held in public, so the scaffold had been erected over a twelve-foot deep pit at one end of the male exercise yard. As Morley stood on the scaffold he became increasingly agitated, but Berry quickly placed a white hood over his head and adjusted the rope around his neck. As the prison chaplain uttered the words 'Lord have mercy upon us', Berry pulled the lever. Morley fell through the trapdoor, and in an instant all was over. Only two minutes had elapsed from the time he entered the yard. Immediately the drop fell a black flag was hoisted on a long flagstaff above the prison governor's office.

The body was left hanging for an hour, as dictated by the rules, then placed in a plain coffin in one of the cells. A reporter noted that Morley 'looked as peaceful as if he had died in bed'. There was an indentation behind his left ear made by the knot in the fatal rope, and the cuts on his hands incurred when he murdered poor Martha Bodger were still plainly visible.

Almost two and a half years later, on 8 February 1890, James Bodger remarried. His new bride was Sarah Turner, a farm labourer's daughter, and the ceremony took place at Chigwell Row Parish Church, where Martha's funeral service had been held. A son, James William, was born to the couple at the end of the same year. Everyone who knew James must have wished him a long and happy life with his new family, but tragically these hopes were to be dashed. On 9 January 1894 he died of influenza at home at Thornwood Common, Epping, aged only 33, and was buried at North Weald.

His daughter Amy, infant witness to the atrocity, proved to be a survivor. She was brought up by her uncle and aunt, Henry and Maria Chambers, at Forest Farm Cottages in Hainault, and was only told of her mother's murder after her own marriage to William Challis in 1912. Amy and her family lived at Osborne Cottages in Ripple Road, Dagenham. In later life she moved to Rainham Road South with her daughter, and on her death at the age of 90 was buried alongside her husband in Dagenham Parish Churchyard.

Sources

Depositions (National Archives, ASSI 36/31)
The *Essex Times*

Chapter 14

Death on New Year's Eve: The Mysterious Case of Mary Jane Voller 1898

I got down on my hands and knees and reached out.
I touched a face, but I could not feel if it was hers.

During the 1890s Barking expanded rapidly to the east of the railway station, into an area which became known as Barking New Town. One of the new streets was Harpour Road, which in late 1898 lay on the very edge of the development. The last house at the northern end of Harpour Road, where it joined Tanner Street, was number 77, home of the Powell family. They had recently let out their upper rooms to Henry Voller, who had just moved into Barking from East Ham with his wife and young children. German-born Mr Voller worked in London as a crane-driver for Messrs Pink, jam manufacturers. His eldest daughter was 5½year old Mary Jane, known as Jennie, who had been born on 19 June 1893 at Custom House.

At about 5.10 p.m. on Saturday, 31 December 1898, Mrs Voller put a threepenny piece into little Mary Jane's hand and sent her to George Wray's corn chandler's shop in Tanner Street for a pennyworth of linseed for making a poultice. When she didn't return within a few minutes, Mrs Voller asked her landlady's daughter Mary Powell to go to the shop and look for her. Mary did so, and reported that the little girl was not there, so Mrs Voller told her husband 'Harry, you had better go and see where Jennie is'. He went out into the damp, foggy night, but on reaching the shop, just over fifty yards

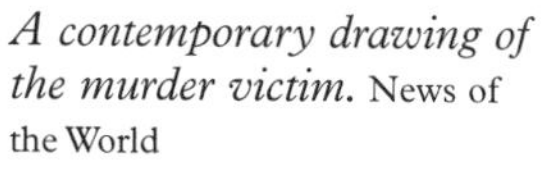

A contemporary drawing of the murder victim. News of the World

away, he was alarmed to hear that his daughter had never arrived there at all. Earlier that day Mr Voller had given the child a penny to spend on herself, so he then looked in nearby sweet shops, but once more found that there had been no sign of her. On returning home he found that she had left her penny behind.

Henry Voller then went to Barking Police Station, in North Street. The sergeant told him to search a while longer, so he walked around Barking, asking people such as the postman whether they had seen her. He then returned to the police station and gave a description of Mary Jane so that it could be circulated. Growing increasingly desperate, he looked for her at the 'show where the roundabouts are' and then went to his father's house to ask for his assistance in the search.

Henry and his father borrowed a lamp from a neighbour, a signalman named Mr Wright. Going out into the rain, they searched some half-built houses on the other side of Harpour Road but without success. Beyond lay a barren area of muddy fields and creeks, awaiting the next stage of

Henry Voller scoured the streets of Barking looking for his daughter. This photograph shows the Broadway in about 1910. LBBD Archives at Valence House Museum

The spot where Mary Jane Voller's body was found. News of the World

building development. Walking along Ilford Lane, shining the lantern around, Henry caught sight of a carpenter's shed near some fence palings which led to a ditch. The spot was close to the Loxford Brook, a tributary of the River Roding, and on the Barking side of the Loxford Bridge. Leaving his elderly father by the road, Henry waded towards the shed through mud and water which reached his knees. As he got to the edge of the ditch he saw something floating in the water.

Henry later reported that:

> *I couldn't see what it was, as just then the light of the lantern went out. I got down on my hands and knees and reached out. I touched a face, but I could not feel if it was hers. I lifted the body out of the water, and then I saw it was my daughter. Her head was resting between her knees. She was dead. I shouted "Father, I've found her".*

Mary Jane was 'doubled up in the water like a ball'. Her head was bent downwards, between her legs, and lay in the mud at the bottom of the water. On pulling her out, Henry found that her mouth and nose were clogged with mud. It was about 7.30 p.m.

Henry's shouts were heard by his wife at their home only about 100 yards away. She rushed to the scene. Her husband wanted to leave the body there and call the police, but the distraught mother said 'No, bring her home, or I shall do so'. Henry accordingly carried Mary Jane in his arms back to Harpour Road, laid her on the floor in front of the fire, then informed the police.

Dr Shimeld of Ilford, the Police Divisional Surgeon, reached the house at about 10.10 p.m. By this time Mary Jane had been undressed and laid on a table. Dr Shimeld noted that some frothy water was coming out of her mouth. She had wounds to her throat and abdomen which though of considerable length barely pierced the skin. There were also two deeper puncture wounds, one on her pelvis about half an inch deep and the other on the inside of her left thigh about three quarters of an inch deep.

Police then took Mary Jane's body to Barking mortuary, where a post-mortem was carried out. It revealed that she had not been sexually assaulted. Meanwhile, detectives from Ilford, Forest Gate, Stratford and Plaistow, under the command of Inspector Mellish, arrived in Barking and began their investigations. Mary Jane's hat was found floating on the water 200 yards from where her body had been discovered. According to the *Barking & East Ham Standard*, a rumour was sweeping the town that 'a child had been ravaged, murdered and thrown into a river...in some cases it went even further by stating that the body had been mutilated and pieces gathered up in different parts'. The *News of the World* billed the case as 'the Barking Horror'.

The inquest on Mary Jane opened the following Tuesday afternoon at Barking Town Hall. The Coroner was Dr Ambrose, and Mr J.W. Garland, greengrocer, was the foreman of the jury. The first witness called was Henry Voller. The *News of the World* reported that he was 'a respectable-looking young fellow, who in a clear and intelligent manner, told the story'. Voller was asked if he could suggest any reason why anyone should do any harm to the child, and replied that he had no enemies that he knew of.

Dr Shimeld was asked for his opinion on the cause of death. He declared that the wounds in themselves were not serious enough to be fatal, yet on the other hand the symptoms of death by drowning were not quite typical – her lungs floated and there was very little water in the stomach. He stated that she seemed to have been unconscious when she entered the water, as she had not attempted to fight or breathe afterwards.

A member of the jury suggested that Mary Jane may have lost her way in the darkness and tumbled over the Loxford Bridge into the water, and had then fainted due to the fright of falling in. Dr Shimeld replied that the shock of falling might indeed have had this effect. When the Coroner asked if he thought the wounds were inflicted by some other person, though, he answered 'Yes, I think so. They were not done by the child herself'. Mr Garland wondered whether they could have been caused by some wire fencing, and another juryman said that timber was sometimes left lying at the riverbank with nails sticking out of it.

The doctor did not think, however, that either of these were likely explanations. In his opinion her wounds had been made deliberately by some sharp instrument such as a penknife or pair of scissors. The latter theory would account for the light scratches seen parallel to the main wounds across Mary Jane's throat and abdomen. The inquest was adjourned to 31 January to allow police time for further extensive enquiries.

The threepenny piece that Mary Jane carried was never found. The *Barking & East Ham Standard* speculated that robbery had been the motive, stating that the only logical conclusion 'is that some dastardly miscreant – and, unhappily, Barking abounds with them on Saturday nights' had decoyed the little girl by some means towards Loxford Bridge. Having robbed her, the culprit had thrown her over the bridge and into the water, the tide carrying the body into the ditch where it was found. The *Standard* continued: 'It was probably done so quickly that the little one could not scream. We cannot see how else it could be done, because at five o'clock in the evening, people are incessantly passing and re-passing along this part of Ilford Lane.'

On the morning of Wednesday, 4 January, some London newspapers put up large placards claiming that a youth had been arrested and had confessed to the murder. This was a 17 year old lad named Pyle, who was known in Barking for his strange behaviour. He had been in the habit of sleeping rough in outhouses, unfinished buildings, and elsewhere. The police had been questioning him as to his movements on the Saturday night, but they did not obtain sufficient evidence to charge him, and he was released on Wednesday evening.

Mary Jane Voller was buried at Rippleside Cemetery on Sunday, 8 January. To prevent large crowds gathering at the scene, her funeral was not announced in advance. On 31 January the adjourned inquest returned a verdict of 'Murder by some person or persons unknown'. Sadly, no one was ever convicted of the crime.

Sources

The *Barking Advertiser*
The *Barking and East Ham Standard*
The *East Ham Echo*
The *News of the World*
The Times

Chapter 15

The Barking Boiler Explosion 1899

The flesh was so scalded and burnt that it disintegrated to the touch.

As the nineteenth century drew to its close William Holmes Frogley, an old inhabitant of Barking and son of a fisherman, wrote regretfully that 'There is very little now in the town to remind us of the old fishing days'. The extension of the railway to ports such as Great Yarmouth and Grimsby had been the chief reason. The deep-sea fishing grounds were situated in the North Sea, and smack owners such as the Hewett family could now send the catch to London by rail direct from the East Coast.

Although Hewett's Short Blue Fleet had long since been relocated to Gorleston, in the year 1899 the firm still maintained a considerable presence in Barking. They had an engineering works on a site between Fisher Street and the River Roding. Fishing smacks and steam-powered trawlers were built, equipped and repaired there. The machines in the various engineering sheds were powered by two boilers – main and auxiliary.

The boiler house was situated roughly in the centre of the complex, and at about 3.15 p.m. on Friday, 6 January 1899 it was the source of a gigantic explosion that shook the whole town and could be heard many miles away. The boiler house itself, blacksmith's shop, offices and other buildings were left in ruins, and a brick stack sixty feet high had crashed down on one of the sheds.

One hundred and twenty men were employed at the works. Rescuers were rapidly on the scene, searching for the injured and pulling them out of the wreckage. It soon became clear that there would be a considerable death toll. *The Times* reported that 'some bodies at the Town Hall Mortuary were so frightfully maimed as to be scarcely recognizable. One

The scene in Hewett's Yard after the explosion. LBBD Archives at Valence House Museum

poor fellow had lost an arm and a leg, another had both legs torn away, and a third was found with the upper part of his head blown off'.

One of the victims was 49 year old Archibald Burness, the foreman fitter and turner. He was discovered still alive but terribly injured, a large piece of wood having crushed his face. He was taken to the Provident Dispensary in the Broadway, but died soon after arriving. Burness, who lived in St Margaret's Road, was a local councillor. He had been widowed less than two years previously, and four of his children were at that time in the Upney Infectious Diseases Hospital suffering from diphtheria.

Two young men who had been working in the boiler house itself were found dead at the scene. They were William Thomas Marshall, 20, who lived in Fisher Street, and Alfred George Frith Grant, an apprentice fitter from East Ham who was just 15 years old. Grant had been working on the boiler at the time of the explosion, and parts of his body were found sixty yards away. Another corpse, which had been blown partly through a wall, was identified as that of George John Pratten, a 50 year old blacksmith from Fisher Street. Close by was the body of Walter Taylor, a hammer man who lived in Boundary Road. A further victim was Edward Lloyd, 57, master of the steamship *Velocity*. He had been at Hewett's to attend a job interview.

At the time the explosion occurred, the organist of St Margaret's Church, Arthur Hume, had been giving an organ lesson to the vicar. The pair then went to Hewetts' works to see what had happened, and Mr Hume was told that his 16 year old son Alfred, an apprentice fitter, was missing. Eventually the boy was found alive, but so badly injured that the doctor told the anguished father that there was no hope. Alfred was taken to his home in Cambridge Road, where he passed away soon afterwards.

Another man pulled from the wreckage in a serious condition was James Thornton, a 40 year old boilermaker. His right leg and left arm were broken. He was taken at speed the three miles to Poplar Hospital, the horse driven so fast that on arrival it was covered with foam and scarcely able to stand. Sadly, Thornton died twenty minutes afterwards. He had lived in St Ann's Road with his wife Clara and their six children.

Another victim taken to Poplar Hospital was John Sullivan, also known as John Shelley. He was only 13 and had just left school. John had been minding a horse outside the *Volunteer* public house about 120 yards from the works when a falling brick struck him on the head. His father James Shelley, having heard the explosion, was making his way towards the scene when he saw some men carrying a boy. One of them said 'Jim, this is your son'. He accompanied John to the hospital, where the boy died on Sunday morning without regaining consciousness. The family lived at Emily Cottages, in Fisher Street.

Eventually all had been accounted for except one – William Page, a 60 year old shipwright who had been working on the steamship *Pelican* at the time of the explosion. Page had been last seen sawing some wood, two minutes before the disaster, by another workman, who had barely escaped with his own life. Captain John Quash and his men of the Barking Volunteer Fire Brigade worked unceasingly to find Page. They were joined in their endeavours by Page's son-in-law, Robert Hammond Tatnell, who worked night and day from Friday afternoon until the following Tuesday, resting only on the Sunday. He cleared large areas of rubble and wreckage during the frantic search. On Tuesday he was joined by the missing man's youngest son Byron Page, and at 2.40 p.m. that day they discovered the body underneath debris in the fitter's shop.

When found, William Page was lying on his left side. His face and head, especially on one side, were terribly crushed and disfigured. The left arm and leg were fractured, the latter being nearly severed at the knee joint, and the ankle dislocated. The lower part of the body was in a ghastly state. His trousers had been blown off altogether, and he was minus even the shoes and socks. The flesh was so scalded and burnt that it disintegrated to the touch. Page's remains were taken to the mortuary by way of Gascoigne Road, to avoid passing his widow's house in Fisher Street. Mrs Page insisted upon seeing the body, and as nothing else would pacify her she was permitted to do so.

Many others were injured. Some were treated at the scene, and others taken to the dispensary in the Broadway. The front room of the dispensary was full of people with broken limbs and wounds to their heads and faces. Some of the more seriously injured were driven to Poplar Hospital in open wagons and carts lent for the purpose.

There was extensive damage to buildings throughout Barking. At the *Fishing Smack*, adjoining the works, landlord Henry Seabrook had been asleep in his back bedroom when he was abruptly awoken by the window frame crashing down on top of him. Luckily he was unhurt, but the pub was very badly damaged. All its front windows were broken, and most of the ceilings had collapsed. A survivor of the explosion, Jim Harden, was dug out of the skittle alley at the *Fishing Smack*. He had been blown through a dividing wall, and was quite disappointed that the blast had not carried him a few yards further into the tap room. Harden was henceforth known locally as 'The Man They Could Not Kill'. Other buildings suffering damage included Messrs Randell's Malt Factory and the *George* in the Broadway.

About 400 yards from the scene of the explosion was Henry Decker's bakery at the corner of Gascoigne Road and Howard Road. A piece of the boiler went clean through the brick wall of the building's upper storey. It then fell through the kitchen ceiling before finally embedding itself a foot into the floor. Luckily for the Decker family, they had just got up from dinner at the kitchen table when the blast occurred.

The crown of the boiler, weighing about a ton, ended up in the back

Sightseers viewing part of the boiler in a field 200 yards from the explosion. News of the World

yard of number 94 Fisher Street, home of the Green family. Mrs Green was taking in her washing when the large piece of iron whizzed by just over her head. It fell right across the back doorway, burying itself about fourteen inches into the ground. Two other pieces fell into the same yard. One was a sheet of iron measuring about 2 feet by 3 feet, which hit a fence and then dropped into the chicken run. The other, an angle iron, fell into the centre of the yard close to Mrs Green and two of her children, who luckily escaped injury. Mr Green arrived home twenty minutes later, and was to tell the *Barking Advertiser* that he 'was greatly surprised to find this large piece of the boiler right across my doorway. It was then still hot'. He dug it out and laid it in his yard. So many sightseers flocked to gaze at it that Mr Green put out a collecting box.

Thousands of people travelled to Barking to view the scene of the explosion, especially on Sunday. Trains were crowded, and roads were jammed with all types of vehicles, from donkey barrows to specially chartered buses running direct from London's East End. Mr Decker's shop was a particular magnet for the sightseers. Police had to be brought in to control the crowds in Fisher Street and Gascoigne Road. They were assisted by Captain Quash and his men, who also collected money for the Calamity Fund. Collecting boxes were placed opposite the works, on tables draped with the Union Jack. Fund-raising events included charity football matches and concerts. The vicar, the Reverend Percy Montague Wathen, and Mr William Wallis Glenny, a prominent local businessman and county councillor, were active in writing to newspapers appealing for aid. Money flowed in from all over the country. William Holmes Frogley noted that £2,085 6s 8d was collected within a year, enabling £200 to be paid to each widow and various other sums to the injured.

The funerals began on Wednesday, 11 January, with the burial of young Alfred Hume. As we have seen, his father was organist at St Margaret's Church, and the lad himself had been a bell-ringer there. The following day, five victims including Councillor Burness were buried at Rippleside Cemetery. Flags flew at half-mast, and business in the town was entirely suspended. Thousands lined the route, braving torrential rain. The procession was led by Barking Police and the Town Band playing the Dead March. On Friday, 13 January, Edward Lloyd and James Sullivan were also laid to rest at Rippleside, while Walter Taylor was buried at East London Cemetery. The funeral of the final victim, William Page, was held the following day. Hewett's paid for all the funerals.

Attention then turned to establishing the cause of the disaster. It was found that the auxiliary boiler had exploded. It was approximately twenty years old, and originally used in a steamship. It had lain unused for several years. The work's manager, Donald Gordon, told the inquest that on Wednesday, 4 January the boiler was being got ready for steam. It was cleaned out and water put in. It was run between the Wednesday and Thursday and reported as being 'all right'. A replacement steam pressure gauge was then fitted. The verdict of the subsequent Board of Trade enquiry was that the explosion had been caused by over-pressure of steam. It was estimated that the pressure rocketed to between 225 and 245 pounds per square inch, the safe limit being only 30 pounds. It was noted

A memorial plaque to the victims of the disaster. Valence House Museum

that Archibald Burness, instead of slackening off the compression nuts of the safety valves, had tightened them instead, thus increasing the pressure.

However, the Board of Trade Commissioners did not attach blame to Burness, as the steam gauge was shown to be faulty and not displaying the correct reading. It judged that Hewett's had failed to employ persons properly qualified to manage the boilers, and had also not taken measures to ensure the boilers were worked under safe conditions. The Board also decreed that Hewett's had breached the rules by not having its boilers regularly examined by Board of Trade inspectors.

As early as 7 January, the day following the disaster, *The Times* reported that Hewett's 'is said not to have been insured, for the business was so extensive and had so many ramifications that it was considered more profitable for the firm to bear its own risk'. Sadly, this turned out to be the case, and Hewett's was unable to pay in full the compensation demanded.

On 12 August 1899 the *Barking Advertiser* reported that Hewett's had submitted a petition for the winding up of the company. Orders had been given for the fishing smacks to return to port and be dismantled at Yarmouth. It was forecast that hundreds of employees would be thrown out of work. A sad end for the once-historic Short Blue Fleet, pride of Barking in the days when the town had been the busiest fishing port in the country.

Sources

The *Barking Advertiser*
The *Barking & East Ham Standard*
The Times
The *News of the World*
Frogley, William Holmes: *Mr Frogley's Barking, a first selection*, edited by Tony Clifford & Herbert Hope Lockwood (2002)
O'Driscoll, Pat: An accident waiting to happen (article in the *Fishing News*, 24 December 1999)

Chapter 16

A Toast to Death 1911

Immediately they tasted the liquid they knew that something was very wrong...

On 3 October 1911 a Frenchman named Ernest Durand was given command of a ship named the *Bouganville*, with orders to take her to the Lawes factory at Creekmouth to be loaded with chemical manure. The vessel, together with its sister ship the *André Théodore*, would then sail to Australia with its less than pleasant but extremely valuable cargo. Captain Durand knew the ship well, having worked on it earlier the same year, and soon made himself at home in the captain's cabin.

The *Bouganville* had been at anchor off Creekmouth for a few days when, on Tuesday, 10 October, a team of inspectors arrived to check the hold and cargo. They were led by Martin Clarke, a shipping manager in his thirties. He was accompanied by G. James Greengrass, a master stevedore aged 64, and 59 year old James Garrard, a Lawes' foreman. The final member of the party was Hubert Austin Rogers Burrough, 36, a City of London stockbroker who lived at Thornton Heath in Surrey. Burrough wasn't there on business but in a purely social capacity, being a friend of Martin Clarke.

Having completed their inspection, the visitors then joined Ernest Durand on board the *Bouganville*, accompanied by Captain Victor Reibillard of the *André Théodore*. Durand asked the others to take a glass of port wine with him to toast the success of the forthcoming voyage. They agreed, and followed him into the captain's cabin. A wine bottle was already open on the table, and the cabin boy brought six glasses. The bottle did not contain enough to go round, so Captain Durand peered into his drinks cupboard in search of more supplies. It contained several bottles, seemingly identical in size, shape and colour. He pulled one out, removed the black wax seal and poured its contents into the six glasses.

The six men raised their glasses, said 'Good health!' and all drank at the same time. Immediately they tasted the liquid they knew that something was very wrong. Their mouths and throats felt as if they were burning, and Durand recalled that 'we experienced terrible pain'. James Garrard screamed 'I'm poisoned!' They scrambled up onto the deck, calling for help, and drank water and lubricating oil in a desperate attempt to quell the burning sensation.

Members of the crew rushed into the Lawes factory, and a telephone call was soon made to Dr John Macdonald of Linton Road, Barking. He hastened to Creekmouth and was rowed out to the *Bouganville*. As Dr Macdonald stepped on board he saw the stricken men lying on the deck. A preliminary examination showed that Hubert Burrough was in a much worse condition than the others. He was unconscious, his face and upper body were a livid colour, and his vital signs were extremely weak. The doctor washed out Burrough's stomach with several pints of warm water, gave him some brandy, and tried artificial respiration.

After about forty-five minutes the patient's breathing was established, and his pulse, though rapid, was fairly good. As the young man seemed to be reviving, he was carefully lowered down over the side to be rowed ashore and sent to hospital. During the few minutes it took to reach the riverbank, however, he died. Clarke, Garrard and Greengrass were also in a serious condition. The Barking Urban District Council's ambulance carried them to Poplar Hospital. Happily they were soon found to be on the mend, and were discharged a few days later. The other two men, the French captains, were not so seriously affected and remained aboard ship under medical supervision.

Burrough's body was taken to the Barking mortuary, and an inquest was held at the Public Offices in East Street four days later, presided over by Coroner Ambrose. Three bottles retrieved from the cupboard in Captain Durand's cabin were placed on a table in front of the coroner and jury. To everyone present the bottles seemed absolutely identical, and even the liquid inside them was of a similar colour. Dr Macdonald revealed,

A ship moored at the Lawes' jetty, Creekmouth, in 1899. LBBD Archives at Valence House Museum

however, that only one contained wine. The other two were found to be full of carbolic acid, although none bore 'Poison' warning labels. The doctor told the jury that Burrough had drunk about half a glass of the liquid, the equivalent of half an ounce of the acid. Such an amount was invariably fatal. Fortunately for the others, they had not imbibed quite so much.

Captain Durand was sufficiently recovered from his ordeal to be able to attend the inquest. He explained that the carbolic acid was carried as a disinfectant. It was supplied as crystals in tins and the captain made it up. Durand declared that his practice was always to put a black seal on the wine bottles and a red one on the disinfectant, and he swore that he always labelled the acid bottles as poisonous, following the regulations. He alleged that the previous captain must have neglected to do this. The inquest jury returned a verdict of accidental death, but added a rider to the effect that there had been great carelessness shown by the previous captain, *or somebody*, in not labelling the bottles properly, or telling the present captain that they contained carbolic acid. The identity of the culprit was never revealed.

Sources

The *Barking Advertiser*
The Times

Chapter 17

The Ajax Factory Disaster 1917

Some were in flames and had to be rolled in the grass to extinguish their burning clothing.

Barking's fishing fleet, as we have seen, had been the town's major employer for hundreds of years but, by the early twentieth century, it had been replaced by a wide range of other industries. By the outbreak of the First World War in 1914 these included Thomas Crow's tar distillery in Harts Lane, R. White's mineral water and lemonade factory in St Paul's Road, and the Vulcan Globe Match Company and William Warne rubber works, both in Abbey Road. In addition there was the Fosbery lifebuoy factory in London Road, which made the lifejackets for the ill-fated liner *Titanic*. The previous year, 1913, the Cape Asbestos factory had been established in Harts Lane. This could be described as a Foul Deed in itself, as it left Barking with the legacy of one of the UK's worst rates of deadly asbestos-related lung disease.

By August 1917, war had been raging for three years. The *Barking Advertiser* marked the anniversary by praising the town's contribution towards the war effort, adding 'not forgetting the sterling work which the women have played throughout'. Many of these women were now taking the places of men in Barking's factories. One hundred and twenty were employed at the Ajax Chemical Works in Hertford Road, Barking, which was contracted to make munitions (explosive shells) for the Admiralty. As the materials used were, by their nature, highly flammable, employees had to wear felt slippers and were banned from bringing in matches. 'Kill Fire' signs and sand buckets were placed around the workrooms. Yet even with these precautions in place, a fire had occurred the previous month, July 1917, destroying a range of brick and corrugated iron buildings with all their contents.

At about 6 p.m. on the evening of Thursday, 9 August seventeen women were at work in an upper room of a two-storey brick and concrete building

Typical female munitions factory workers during the First World War. Authors' collection

about 60 feet wide and 100 feet long. Staff were changing shifts, and among those getting ready to leave were 45 year old Mrs Martha Gurry, and Ada Waters, who sat with her at the workbench. Mrs Gurry's 15 year old son, Charles Panons, was employed by Ajax to carry chemical powders and mixtures from one place to another. Charles had visited that particular workroom from time to time during the day, and returned to give his mother some dinner things before she left. He then went out, and immediately afterwards Ada Waters heard a dull thud behind her and was aware of smoke rising from the corner of the room. Suddenly there was a huge blast. Ada was blown down the staircase, and the next thing she knew she was in the yard with her clothes alight.

Christopher Cox, an assistant manager of the works, said he heard 'a dull sound similar to a box of matches going off'. Others agreed that it was 'a soft noise, more like a sudden burst of air rather than an explosion'. The workroom windows were iron-framed and opened outwards. Three people jumped ten feet to the ground, and one was taken to hospital due to the injuries that she sustained. Dense dark blue smoke came streaming out, followed instantly by a fierce blaze shooting through the windows and roof. The smoke gave off extremely noxious fumes.

Mr Cox immediately ran into the building, but there was another explosion and the door slammed behind him. Trapped inside, he was on the point of being overcome by the smoke when the chief chemist managed to open the door and rescue him. Workers rushed out at the same time. Some were in flames and had to be rolled in the grass to extinguish their burning clothing. The Barking Fire Brigade was called at 6.05 p.m. and left three minutes later, but was delayed when the fire engine had a wheel wrenched off in a tramline at Bull Corner. When it arrived at the scene at 6.19 p.m. the East Ham Brigade was already at work.

Captain Edward James Abbott, Barking's Chief Fire Officer, entered the blazing building but was driven back. He then made another attempt, and this time got up the stairs and returned with a body. He tried yet again and brought out two others. Abbott then put on a smoke helmet and pulled out another six bodies before collapsing from the effect of the chemical fumes. The *Barking Advertiser* stated that 'it is impossible to speak in adequate terms of the bravery and courage and self-sacrificing devotion to duty shown by Chief Officer Abbott…it would be hard to find a parallel at any fire to his stupendous work amid terrifying scenes'. He was awarded the King's Police Medal for his actions.

The Barking Fire Brigade retained horse-drawn vehicles until 1922. A similar scene to this would have occurred as the horses galloped towards the scene of the Ajax factory disaster. LBBD Archives at Valence House Museum

When the fire was eventually extinguished, the whole top floor of the building had been burnt out, together with one end of the ground floor and an adjoining engine-house. The main premises were relatively undamaged. A total of thirteen charred bodies were found, in two heaps near the exits at either end of the room. It seemed that as the women ran to the stairs, some must have fallen, others tripping over them. Before they could get up they were overcome by the smoke and fumes. One had her hands at her throat, showing that she was struggling against suffocation.

When the inquest opened in the Council Chamber at the Public Offices (now the Magistrates' Court), the coroner's first task was to hear evidence of identification. This was a difficult process, as the intense fire had almost destroyed the bodies and clothing. The mother of Gladys B. Knight, 17, from Manor Park, identified her by the contour of her face and the way she did her hair at the back. Mrs Knight fainted after giving her evidence, and had to be carried from the room. Ellen Rainbow, aged 16, of Hardwicke Street, Barking, was also identified by her mother, who recognized two teeth. Another young victim was Ada Clarke, aged 18, from Manor Park, whose father William Horace Clarke recognized a piece of tape he had previously noticed round her waist.

Most of the dead women were married and had families. Two sisters, Mrs Edith Maskell, 37, and Mrs Rose Abbott, 32, both of Caulfield Road, East Ham, were found lying together. Mrs Maskell's husband identified her by a portion of the blouse which she wore, and also recognized Mrs Abbott by her false teeth. Ellen Webb, 45, from East Ham, was identified by her wedding ring, and Catherine England, 43, from Upton Park, by part of one of her boots. Mary Ann Foley, 49, from East Ham, had a slight deformity of one of her toes. Martha Gurry, the supervisor of the room, also died. The other victims were Sarah King, 37 year old Mary Ellen Smith, and Mary Ann Pearson (known as Mrs Pennell), all from East Ham, and Alice Cole, 31, of Howard Road, Barking.

The Deputy Coroner, Mr Frank Collins, said 'he was pretty hardened in things he had seen, but this was one of the worst cases he had had to hold an inquest upon'. He declared that there had been 'no possibility of rescue alive amidst the insuperable difficulties that surrounded the calamity'. Following legal advice, the disaster was referred to as a 'fire' rather than as an 'explosion'. Apparently there had been no lack of other escape routes. The jury then retired for about forty-five minutes and brought in a verdict of 'accidental death through suffocation caused by a fire, the origin or cause of which remained unknown'.

An incident described at the inquest might hold the clue to the mystery. The lad Charles Panons, who delivered the chemical powders to the areas where the munitions were assembled, and who had left the workroom just seconds before the catastrophe occurred, also helped to mix the substances. He told the inquest that on the day of the disaster he and John Pawley, the foreman mixer, were preparing a mixture that was new to them. He said that he removed the iron lid of one container only to find that a piece of the substance inside, about the size of a fingernail, had caught alight. It burned for a moment 'like a match-head', and he thought that friction caused by moving the lid had possibly been the cause. Pawley, the foreman, had then told him 'Look out, Charley! You see how dangerous it is'. Pawley in turn explained to the coroner that he had reported the incident to the chemist, who had said 'You mix it as I tell you, and it will be all right'.

Just before 1 p.m. Panons had taken the new mixture up to the room where the fire was to occur five hours later. Is it more than coincidence that the fire broke out immediately after he had been to the room to see his mother, Martha Gurry, who was to become one of the victims? Did he inadvertently create some friction or disturbance that ignited the volatile chemicals of the untried new mixture?

Some victims were wives of men away on active service. One soldier husband, a father of nine, arrived home as the inquest was proceeding. The husband of Sarah King happened to return on leave from the Western Front on the very evening of the disaster. He had last seen his wife alive on 25 June when she saw him off at Waterloo Station. On getting home on 9 August, with the trench mud still upon him, he was told that half an hour previously his wife's charred body had been brought out of the burning building. The shocked man was then asked to identify her, and reported that he could tell it was his wife by one of the fingers and the nail on it. No doubt Sarah had always been anxious for his welfare amidst the carnage of the Front, but fate decreed that she would lose her life and he, this time, would return safely home.

Sources

The *Barking Advertiser*
The Times
The *East Ham Echo*
The *Barking Chronicle*

Chapter 18

The Becontree Murder: Grace Newing 1933

When asked what was the matter, he told her, 'I have done Gracie in'.

After the First World War the London County Council purchased land in Barking, Dagenham and Ilford as part of its Homes for Heroes programme, and in 1921 work began on building the huge Becontree Estate. By the early 1930s it consisted of over 25,000 houses, making it the largest council estate in the world. Dagenham, previously a rural parish, was now home to huge numbers of people, mainly ex-East Enders.

A typical young couple moving to Becontree were Charles William Kirby, a fireman, and his wife Hannah, who must have been delighted to take possession of a brand new home in Valence Circus in the mid-1920s. A few years later they agreed to accommodate his mother Sarah Jane and younger brother Robert James Kirby. Robert, known as Bob, had been born in March 1907 at 13 Sidmouth Road, Leyton. His mother described him as a quiet boy, not a good achiever at school, who 'would not make friends with anyone, but led a solitary life'. Robert's absent father, Charles Kirby, had been sentenced to four years' penal servitude for attempting to murder his wife. On leaving school Robert drifted into petty crime and was sent to prison three times for housebreaking. He joined the army with his younger twin brothers but was asked to leave 'due to his character'.

In spring 1933, 26 year old Robert, who had been unemployed for some time, began a relationship with Grace Ivy Newing, ten years younger than himself. Grace also lived on the Becontree Estate, in Stevens Road, together with her mother and several younger brothers and sisters. Her parents, George and Rosina Newing, had separated. Grace was

Valence Circus, home of the Kirby family, photographed in about 1945 LBBD Archives at Valence House Museum

described in the *Dagenham Post* as 'pretty in appearance, and vivacious, she was helping her mother to keep the home going'. She had been born in Park Grove, Battersea, on 1 July 1916, a date forever associated with the tragic loss of life on the first day of the Battle of the Somme.

Grace had until recently worked at a local cinema, but now had a job in a confectioner's shop at 924 Romford Road, Manor Park. On Thursday evenings she would work late, sometimes until 11 p.m., and Kirby would either wait for her at her home or go and meet her. On the night of Thursday, 6 July, five days after Grace's seventeenth birthday, Kirby arrived at her house in Stevens Road as usual, at about 8.45 p.m. Her mother went to bed about two hours later, leaving Robert waiting for Grace to come in. Three days previously he had confided to Mrs Newing that he thought Grace was pregnant, and that he was 'willing to stand by her'.

Just over two hours later, at about 1 a.m., Robert's mother Sarah Jane, sleeping in her room at the Valence Circus house, was suddenly awoken by the touch of a cold hand on her arm. It was Robert, 'very white. He looked like a statue'. When asked what was the matter, he told her 'I have done Gracie in'. She cried in disbelief 'You haven't, Bob!' but he replied 'I have, Mum'. His brother Charles came in and asked 'What's the matter with you?' and Robert repeated 'I've done Gracie in'. He then announced 'I'm going to Ilford to give myself up', and left the house.

Charles Kirby quickly got dressed, took out his bicycle and cycled away along Green Lane, which led to Ilford, but there was no sign of his brother. He then made his way to the nearest police station, which was at

A modern view of Stevens Road, Dagenham Authors' collection

Chadwell Heath, arriving at 2.15 a.m. PC John Bird was on duty, and on hearing the story decided to go immediately to the Newing house at Stevens Road. About fifteen minutes later Mrs Newing was roused from sleep by knocking at the door. PC Bird and Charles Kirby preceded her to a room at the back of the house used as a combined sitting room and kitchen. The room was in darkness, so Bird switched on his electric lamp. The beam illuminated a figure lying partly on the sofa and partly on the floor. It was a young woman, and Bird reported that 'It was quite plain to me that she was dead'. Mrs Newing was standing behind him, and just caught a glimpse of her daughter before Bird ushered her back out of the room.

At about 2.55 a.m. Dr Matthew Frew arrived and began to examine the body. He judged that Grace had been dead between two and three hours. Rigor mortis had not yet set in. Her right arm was bent, the hand level with the top of the head, and she held a handkerchief in her left hand. Her left leg was straight, and the other bent up so that her right foot and ankle were tucked under her left leg. Deeply embedded in her neck was a green cord, of the kind used for hanging pictures. It was knotted at the front.

Dr Frew reported that her clothes were pulled up and her knickers torn. 'Her face was swollen and the eyes partly protruding. There was a little blood and froth coming from the left side of the mouth. There were no signs of a struggle.' He later carried out a post-mortem which confirmed that she had died from strangulation and had been four weeks' pregnant. There were no marks on her body apart from those on the neck.

Meanwhile, Robert Kirby had changed his mind about giving himself up at Ilford Police Station. Instead, he headed for the house of his brother Francis at Westdown Road, Leyton. He arrived about 6.20 a.m. and asked for a wash and a cup of tea. His freedom was not to last much longer. About half an hour later there was a knock at the door and two police officers entered, one of whom announced that he was Detective Inspector Alexander Lawrence and that he had come to arrest Kirby on suspicion of murder. Kirby replied 'I have nothing to say, let's go!'

The officers drove Kirby to Chadwell Heath Police Station, where he made no attempt to deny the charge. When bloodstains were found on his shirt and braces, he said 'Yes, that came from the girl's nose'. A mysterious note was found on him, written in Grace's writing on the flap of an envelope. It read:

> *I am sorry. You can go. It won't make any difference. He is going just the same. It is useless trying to reconcile us. Besides, I have other things to think of. Grace.*

When this was shown to Mrs Newing she said she had not the slightest idea what it was about. She had always thought Grace and Kirby had a good relationship, with no trouble or disagreements between them.

A few hours after his arrest, Kirby was handcuffed and put into a police van for the journey to Stratford Magistrates' Court, accompanied by PC Henry Preston. As they passed through Manor Park Kirby pointed to a shop and said grimly 'That's where she worked; they will be unlucky if they think she is coming in today'. He told Preston 'I know what my lot will be, and the quicker the better'. He said that while walking to his brother's house in Leyton he would occasionally see a police car go by, and each time he thought 'This is my lot'. He claimed he could not get a job because of his criminal record, and that it seemed impossible for him to marry Grace and provide for a home and family. He then allegedly admitted 'I was not going to let anyone else have her'. However, Kirby then changed his story, claiming that Grace had repeatedly asked him to kill her, and had even carried the cord about with her in her handbag. The Stratford magistrates remanded him in custody at Brixton Prison for a week.

On the afternoon of Thursday, 13 July, a week after Grace's death, her burial took place at the cemetery adjoining St Mary's Church in Ilford. Large crowds stood in the pouring rain waiting for the arrival of the hearse. There was a short service inside the church before the interment of Grace's coffin. Amidst the numerous wreaths and floral tributes there were two from Robert Kirby's family – one from his mother and another from his brothers.

The following morning, 14 July, Kirby again appeared before the Stratford magistrates. A crowd of people, chiefly women, were waiting in the entrance hall, and when Kirby was brought into court there were scuffles as they pushed forward in the hope of getting in. The police had to eject most of the crowd and shut the doors before proceedings could get under way. Kirby's mother was one of the first witnesses to be called. Described as a 'pitiful figure…worn and pale…voice overcome at times with emotion', she told the court of being awoken by her son on the night of the murder. She was almost inaudible at times, seemingly on the verge of collapse, and sipped from a glass of water.

Grace's mother, Rosina Newing, was dressed in deep mourning and cut an equally tragic figure. She said she had not heard Grace come in that evening, and had been unaware of any shouting or signs of a struggle or disturbance during the night. Grace's 11 year old brother George stated that he and a friend had been playing in the garden that day with some long lengths of the green cord, and had left one piece on the arm of the sofa and another in a dresser drawer. The hearing took two hours, after which Kirby was remanded for a further week. Finally, on 21 July, it was ruled that Kirby would face trial at the Central Criminal Court.

Two months later he stepped into the Old Bailey dock and pleaded not guilty to murder. The jury, of whom three were women, were shown the cord which had been tied around Grace's throat, her mysterious note, her underwear, Kirby's bloodstained shirt, and a plan of the Stevens Road house. The defence made much of the fact that Grace did not appear to have put up any resistance, although she was 'a strong, well-made girl, and powerful'. Dr Matthew Frew stated that 'There was no evidence of any connection when I examined her', presumably meaning that she had not recently had sex. He also told the court that Grace had 'a persistent thymus gland, a condition which might cause death by strangulation to occur more easily than it would in a normal person'.

The defence barrister Mr Travers Peregrine put forward evidence in favour of Kirby being insane and thus not responsible for his actions. It seemed that Kirby had made two suicide attempts within the past year. After swallowing ear-drops he had been sent to Clark's Croft Mental Deficiency Institution for twelve days, but had subsequently taken forty-nine aspirin tablets. When asked why, he had merely said he was 'fed up'. A mental health specialist, Dr E. Caldwell-Smith, said he thought Kirby had 'a definite defect of reason' and seemed to think he had done the right thing in killing Grace. Apparently Kirby had told him 'The girl asked me to do it...she wished to die and I did her the favour...I would do anything for her'. Kirby, he added, 'affected a silly grin while talking about the case'.

The Brixton Prison doctor, Hugh Grierson, told the jury that he found Kirby 'of a sullen disposition – he has a habit of grinning, especially when spoken to'. Unlike Dr Caldwell-Smith, however, he did not believe Kirby was insane: 'his conduct and conversation have been rational...He behaved as the majority of men do on a serious charge'. The court adjourned for twenty minutes while Mr Peregrine vainly attempted to get Kirby to speak in his own defence. He felt that the jury should see and hear the accused man for themselves, 'as the question of insanity is not decided either by prison doctors or Harley Street specialists'. But Kirby would not budge. The *Dagenham Post* noted that he 'retained an indifferent calm. He gave the impression that he did not care what happened to him'.

On Thursday, 21 September 1933 the jury retired to consider their verdict. After deliberating for only a quarter of an hour they returned, and the foreman announced: 'We find him guilty of murder, with a recommendation to mercy'. The judge, Mr Justice Swift, asked Kirby if he had anything to say before sentence was passed. In 'a voice clear and composed' he replied 'No'. The judge then donned the black cap and pronounced the sentence of death by hanging. Watchers noted that Kirby still retained his composure. 'Only once did his calm desert him while the Judge was speaking the fateful words. For a fraction of a second his body sagged and his eyes closed. The next moment he was as calm as ever.' He even smiled slightly as he was being led out of the dock.

It was announced that Kirby would be executed three weeks later, pending further reports on his mental state. These did not convince the Home Office to grant him a reprieve, and on Tuesday, 10 October it was announced that he would be hanged the next day inside Pentonville Prison. The following morning a notice was posted outside the prison gates confirming that the execution had taken place.

Because Kirby would not give his side of the story in court, we are left to speculate about his motives. What was the meaning of the cryptic note? Does it imply that Grace was seeing someone else, seeking a partner who could offer her and her child a more financially secure future? Was Kirby therefore telling the truth when he said to PC Preston 'I was not going to let anyone else have her'? It seems inconceivable that Grace had asked him to kill her, or that she would agree to a suicide pact. Bearing in mind that there was no sign of a struggle, could it have been a sex game that went terribly wrong?

Kirby had twice attempted suicide. His mental state was obviously very fragile, and he exhibited an unnatural composure during his trial. In 1933 he was judged to be of sound enough mind to be executed, but perhaps society would have taken a different view today.

Sources

The *Dagenham Post*
Indictment (National Archives, CRIM 4/1582)
Depositions (National Archives, CRIM 1/659)

Chapter 19

The Colditz Rat: Walter Purdy

...being asked his place of birth, he replied, 'Barking, and true British and never would be anything else'.

Only four British citizens were convicted of high treason after the Second World War, the most well-known being William Joyce, the pro-Nazi broadcaster 'Lord Haw-Haw', hanged in 1946. The community in Barking must have been shocked to discover that one of the infamous quartet, Walter Purdy, was a local man. Purdy, grandson of a Barking fisherman, had been born in May 1918 at 270 Boundary Road, and baptized at St Margaret's Church. His father Edward Purdy, a dock worker, died before the mid-1930s. Mrs Alice Purdy and her younger children, including Walter, moved to Westrow Drive. Walter grew up to be 5 feet 8 inches tall with blue eyes and fair hair, and when still a teenager became a member of the Ilford branch of the British Union of Fascists.

Purdy joined the Merchant Navy as an engineer, and on the outbreak of war in 1939 was transferred to the Royal Navy. Purdy's ship, HMS *Van Dyck*, was sunk in the summer of 1940 off Norway and he became a prisoner of war. Purdy was in the Marlag POW Camp from about July 1941 to May 1943, and while there he bought William Joyce's book *Twilight over England* from a guard. Purdy had, it seems, known Joyce before the war through his British Union of Fascists activities. Purdy had made himself unpopular with fellow inmates by telling wild stories, for example claiming that his sister was married to a lord and presented at Court. He was described as 'offensive and quarrelsome'.

The Germans, however, saw potential in Purdy's fascist leanings. On 10 May 1943 he was sent to Stalag IIID/999, near Berlin, a so-called 'holiday camp' for prisoners of war identified as likely collaborators.

Purdy now re-encountered William Joyce, who persuaded him to begin broadcasting for Radio National 208.6, a station based in Berlin but pretending to originate in Britain. Sound engineer Herbert Krumbiegel later praised Purdy as 'the most enthusiastic worker on the Radio National station'. Purdy used the pseudonym Pointer, and wrote his scripts under the direction of the German Foreign Office Propaganda Department. Yet he introduced his broadcasts with 'This is British Radio National – the only entirely uncensored radio station run by Englishmen'. His programmes displayed a heavily anti-Semitic tone in keeping with Nazi propaganda. On 23 July 1943, for example, he declared 'We have no quarrel with the Germans…our fight is here at home. Our fight is against the corrupt, Jew-suborned government which has betrayed the true interests of the people'.

Purdy was allowed to go wherever he liked in Berlin without an escort, and live in a private house in the Reichstrasse. He was paid 400 Reichsmarks per month. He kept a diary for a while, revealing private opinions that were extremely pro-German. On Sunday, 30 January 1944, for example, he mentioned 'English terror bombers' and two weeks later he wrote: 'The blasted RAF came and gave the Reichhauptstelle a pasting'. He would also sign off his letters with 'Heil Hitler'.

George Carpenter, an RAF officer who met Purdy a few times during this period, said that he was 'a most conceited and loud-mouthed individual'. Purdy told Carpenter 'he was a first-class broadcaster and was much sought after by other German radio stations, and added that he was known as the Man with the Golden Voice'. Purdy was, however, later removed from propaganda broadcasting and given a news reading job. Another Englishman who encountered Purdy at this time was told:

> *I'm no longer English, my name is no longer Purdy. I've got my papers changed and am German now. I'm going to marry a German girl in about three days' time.*

This young lady was Margarete Weitemeier, who met Purdy in November 1943. Purdy told Margarete that his name was Robert, or Bob, Wallace. His love of aliases is also shown by letters to his mother in which he signs as Roy.

Purdy's comfortable life in Berlin ended abruptly in March 1944 when he was sent to Oflag IVC, the infamous Colditz maximum security prison for persistent escapers. As was routine, he was interviewed by high-ranking British officers shortly after arrival. They had already heard rumours about his German sympathies, and were suspicious about why he had been sent there. If Purdy attempted to bluff his way through the interview, his pretence did not last long. Colonel William Tod, the Senior British Officer at Colditz, demanded to know whether it was true he had worked for the Germans. Purdy replied 'Yes, I have been a traitor and a rat', and admitted broadcasting. He went on to say that if he were allowed to go back to his girlfriend in Berlin on condition that he worked for the Germans again, he'd agree without hesitation. It seems that at this point Purdy was court-martialled by the British POWs and condemned to death. Colonel Tod told the German Kommandant that he could not be responsible for Purdy's life if he remained. Purdy was accordingly transferred to the punishment cells after spending only forty-eight hours in the camp compound.

Yet even in his short time in Colditz Purdy had gathered two pieces of important information which, it seems, he immediately communicated to the Germans. He had heard talk about John Henry Owen Brown, who had been appointed by the Germans as manager of the 'holiday camp' Stalag IIID. Purdy learned that Brown was doing 'pretty good stuff' by gathering intelligence for the British security services. This was true, and after the war Brown was awarded the Distinguished Conduct Medal. The Germans, it seems, did not believe Purdy's allegations. The second piece of information passed on by Purdy was the location of an escape tunnel from which he had seen a man emerge. The day after Purdy was sent to the punishment cell the guards raided the tunnel, seizing a hoard of escape equipment and a wireless set. Previous searches had failed to locate the tunnel, but this time the Germans went straight there.

By June 1944 Purdy had returned to Berlin. He had written a letter from Colditz to the British Free Corps, a unit of British and Commonwealth ex-POWs who now fought for Hitler on the Eastern Front, wearing an SS uniform which featured a Union Jack on its left sleeve. They had been recruited using a mixture of blackmail, bribery and intimidation. Purdy wrote that he was a long-standing member of the Fascist movement and believed in the struggle against Bolshevism. He stated that he wished to join the British Free Corps as an officer. Consequently from November of that year he worked as an English interpreter for 'Skorpion West', the propaganda section of the SS. He later claimed to have sung on two records while working for them, and it was alleged that he asked to take German nationality in February 1945.

In April 1945 Purdy was sent to Italy to do similar propaganda work. The war in Europe was now drawing to a close, and when the Germans surrendered in May, he made his way to Allied lines, telling them he had escaped from enemy hands. Purdy was repatriated to Britain on 25 May 1945, and on 3 October was discharged from the Armed Forces suffering from neurosis. His wartime activities were about to catch up with him, for on 6 October MI5 sent a letter to the Director of Public Prosecutions, detailing his career on Radio National and his suspected betrayal of John Brown.

Purdy, now aged 27, had moved to Burstock Road, Putney and was working as a salesman for an engineering firm. On 14 October 1945 he had gone to hospital, still wearing Navy uniform, complaining of 'visual hallucinations' and 'mental blackout'. He declared that he had spent eighteen months in solitary confinement, and had endured captivity in Berlin during the heaviest Allied air raids. He was diagnosed with acute anxiety. Two days later he was arrested at Putney Bridge Road and taken to Bow Street Police station. While having his fingerprints taken, and being asked his place of birth, he replied 'Barking, and true British and never would be anything else'. He was then sent to Brixton Prison.

During that summer of 1945 Purdy had met Irene Betty Blaney, 31, a telephonist, of Wharncliffe Gardens, London. Introducing himself as Bob Purdy, he took her out to restaurants and theatres. For some reason, he had given Irene two signed statements confessing his traitorous behaviour, but she threatened to pass them to a newspaper unless he paid her £50. Mrs Blaney was later convicted of blackmail.

Purdy appeared at Bow Street Magistrates' Court on 18 October 1945 on a charge of committing high treason. He pleaded not guilty. He was remanded in custody, then on his next appearance committed for trial at the Old Bailey. He faced three charges – broadcasting for the enemy, giving information to the enemy while a POW and preparing pamphlets and leaflets for German propaganda.

Purdy asserted that 'my actions were one hundred per cent patriotism and that I'm not guilty of High Treason'. His defence rested on three claims. He said he only agreed to make the broadcasts on being assured that he would be allowed to escape to a neutral country after making ten programmes within ten weeks. He wanted to obtain his freedom so that he could fight for the Allies once more.

Purdy's second claim was that he 'was able to render real aid to the RAF bombing campaign'. This was done mainly by coded references in weekly letters to his mother and sister Millicent, who lived near each other in Westrow Drive, Barking. His sister's nephew, Eric, was an RAF apprentice and, in his letters to her, Purdy used the name Eric to signify the RAF bombers. He would write 'Eric has been over again', or 'Have Eric's employers got the information I sent?' Millicent told the court that she sent the letters mentioning Eric to the War Office. His mother was also a witness, and spoke about odd letters with codes and poems in them.

Purdy also claimed that when broadcasting he used a code indicating different weather conditions over Berlin. This was achieved by adding different endings to his programmes. He said that he usually signed off with 'Goodnight' or 'Goodnight all', but that if the weather was suitable for launching an air raid he would say 'Goodnight everybody goodnight'. The Air Ministry, however, dismissed this claim, and it was also pointed out that the broadcasts were pre-recorded. Purdy further declared that he had paid money for information on flak defences of Berlin to pass on to Allied bombers.

Purdy's third line of defence was that he had been able to help his country by acts of sabotage. He said that with the assistance of a Frenchman named Gadeau he carried out about twenty attacks on German targets. On 7 September 1943, for example, he claimed to have thrown a petrol bomb into the Night Fighter HQ at the Terrace Café, Reichsportfeld. Three months later, he said, he obtained twenty hand grenades and blew up a bridge over a road at Tiergarten railway station. What is more, he declared that he loathed William Joyce and had twice tried to kill him – once by throwing a hand-grenade into a railway carriage in which Joyce was travelling (it apparently failed to go off), and the second time by planning to lob a hand-grenade at Joyce when he opened his front door. Purdy alleged he had been court-martialled by the Germans and sentenced to death for espionage and for attempting to murder Joyce.

Purdy claimed that in March 1944 he had tried to escape from Berlin by attempting to obtain a rail pass to go to Austria for medical treatment. From there he had intended to go on to neutral Sweden. He said the Gestapo had raided his flat on 7 March and immediately sent him to Colditz. He also alleged that he was beaten by the Germans in June 1944 until he agreed to resume working for them by helping to create the SS propaganda leaflets to be dropped on British troops. He claimed to have deliberately put errors in the leaflets.

Purdy's German girlfriend Margarete Weitemeier was flown from Berlin to give evidence, but kept in Holloway Prison for the duration of the trial as an enemy alien. Margarete told the court that she didn't know what Purdy's work in Berlin involved. She stated that he was always pro-British, and that she herself was anti-Nazi. She said the couple had wanted to marry, but the Gestapo forbade it as he was English, and that they had both been arrested in March 1944. Newspapers described Margarete as slim and dark-eyed, but failed to mention that she and Purdy had a son, Stephan, who had been born 5 April 1945.

After hearing the evidence, the Old Bailey jury were absent for seventeen minutes then returned to give their verdicts. Purdy was found guilty on the charges of broadcasting and of editing SS pamphlets. He was acquitted on the more serious charge of giving information to the enemy about the secret tunnel and wireless set at Colditz, and the activities of John Brown. He was sentenced to death by hanging. His sister Millicent screamed 'My God! My God!' on hearing the verdict, fainted and had to be carried out of the courtroom by police.

An appeal for clemency was submitted, and the day before Purdy was due to be hanged, his sentence was reduced to life imprisonment. The authorities evidently considered that Purdy was not in the same league as William Joyce. In a letter dated 20 October 1945, Joyce's wife Margaret summed him up in these words:

Purdy's dotty of course – pity I can't give evidence because almost as soon

Air Raid wardens (and dog!) based at Eastbury House during World War Two. Some of the many inhabitants of Barking and Dagenham making a vital contribution to the war effort, while Walter Purdy was following a different route. LBBD Archives at Valence House Museum

> *as he was out of the camp he told me he'd made a mistake and he was worried because he thought he was a traitor – he didn't have much brains but what he had were in a whirl all the time!*

Purdy was released from jail after serving nine years, and died in 1982. Much of the evidence at his trial was kept secret until the release of official papers on his case in the year 2000. The report on the files in the *Sunday Times* on 12 November 2000 began 'He was the rat of Colditz', and continued:

> *As British prisoners of war dug tunnels and built gliders to help them escape from the castle, Walter Purdy, a naval lieutenant, was tipping off their German captors. Newly released files from MI5…give details of the extent of his betrayal…Kenneth Lockwood, a former army captain imprisoned at the castle for four years and secretary of the 54-strong*

Colditz Association of remaining former inmates, said: 'Even the German army officer in charge of security at Colditz told us after the war that he did not approve of Purdy'.

Sources

Case files (National Archives, KV 2/259, KV 2/260, KV 2/261)
West, Rebecca: *The meaning of treason* (1949)
Weale, Adrian: *Renegades: Hitler's Englishmen* (1994)

Chapter 20

The Watchmaker's Wallet: Percy Busby 1947

He told me we could easily shove him over and get the dough.

Barking, in common with many other British towns, was left in a sorry state when the Second World War ended in 1945. More than 200 residents had died in air raids, and thousands of homes were either destroyed or seriously damaged. The post-war housing shortage caused hundreds of families to squat in Nissen huts formerly used by the military. Even basic foods such as bread and meat continued to be rationed.

A familiar sight in Barking in those days was the figure of 55 year old Percy Busby going about the bomb-scarred streets in his hand-propelled wheelchair. Busby had lived there for over thirty years, firstly in Keith Road and then at 11 King Edward's Road, near the *Westbury Arms* pub.

The junction of Ripple Road (on the left) and King Edward's Road, photographed in 1973. Percy Busby's home (now demolished) was just to the right of the picture LBBD Archives at Valence House Museum

He was unmarried. His friends included 'Chick', a one-legged man who sold newspapers outside the railway station, and Rachel Holt, a neighbour who would invite him to her home on Christmas Day and look after his two cats whenever he was in hospital.

Busby was only 5 feet 4 inches tall, and when he did try to walk he was bent almost double. In spite of his frail appearance, however, he had a strong upper body, and had been known to lift bags of metal weighing up to 85lbs. He would carry his wheelchair over the front doorstep, and had even been seen to haul an iron bedstead upstairs. Busby's occupation was repairing clocks and watches but, by the autumn of 1947, he was only doing this in a small way as replacement springs were in short supply. His main activity now was collecting scrap lead and copper wire from rubbish dumps at Creekmouth. He would carry it back to Barking on his wheelchair and earn up to £9 per week selling it.

One of Busby's associates was 32 year old Walter Leslie Bull, known as Leslie, who would visit him about once a week to do small odd jobs or sell him items such as clocks and silver. Busby thought highly of Bull and would sometimes lend him small amounts of money. Bull lived with his wife and child in Levine Gardens on the Scrattons Farm Estate, just south of Ripple Road. He was a decorator by trade but in October 1947 was out of work. He had three convictions for theft.

Bull had a 21 year old friend named Walter John Cross, known as Ginger. Cross had been born in Barking, and his first job on leaving Cambell School was as delivery boy for Mr Pike, a shoe repairer of Longbridge Road. He later worked at Lakeside Ironworks in Ripple Road and at Victor Blagden paints, also in Barking. Cross had been convicted twice for theft. In August 1947 he married his pregnant girlfriend, and the couple moved into her parents' home in Orchard Road, Dagenham, not far from Shaw Avenue, where Cross had previously lived with his mother.

Towards the end of October 1947 the Labour Exchange arranged a job interview for Leslie Bull at Delta Shoes. This was not far from Percy Busby's house in King Edward's Road, so Bull decided to call in on the way. He invited Cross to go with him. Cross was also unemployed. He had left his a job as a lorry driver with Marcan of Barking on 10 October due to a recurrence of a shoulder complaint that had caused him to be discharged from the Army in August 1944 after only four months' service. Busby welcomed the pair inside and made them some tea. When Bull asked him how he was getting on with the copper wire, Busby replied 'No good, they've stopped me going there'.

About three weeks later, on Wednesday, 12 November, Bull and Cross returned. Bull brought along a shirt, scarf and plastic tablecloth and Busby agreed to buy them for 12s 6d, no questions asked. From the hip pocket of his trousers Busby pulled out an old brown leather wallet, bulging with banknotes. He offered a £1 note to Bull, who had no change but rose to get some from a nearby grocer's shop. Just as he was about to leave, there came a knock on the door. It was Rachel Holt, Busby's kindly neighbour. Bull obtained the change, and the two young men then left.

Busby slept in the downstairs front room of his house. He usually let out both upstairs bedrooms but at that time there was only one lodger, Albert Harris. On Friday, 14 November 1947 Harris came in at 7.30 p.m. and joined Busby in the kitchen. The weekly rent of fourteen shillings was due, so Harris handed over a £1 note. Busby grabbed it and pretended to throw it into the fire. Sometimes the pair would spend the evening playing cards, but on this occasion Harris, who worked shifts as a night watchman for Berry & Sons of Westbury Road, decided to go straight to bed. With a 'Goodnight Perc', he went upstairs, shut his bedroom door and soon fell asleep.

Over an hour later, at about 8.50 p.m., Mrs Doris Robinson was walking down King Edward's Road when she noticed a man in front of Busby's house, looking up at the windows. It was raining hard, and the man wore a raincoat with the collar up. As she passed by, she looked at him, and he made a signal with his thumb as though to say 'Clear off'. He wore a cap with the peak pulled down, and seemed anxious to keep his face away from her.

About forty minutes later, at 9.30 p.m., Busby's neighbour, Mrs Florence Wright of number 13, was painting one of her kitchen cupboards when she heard sounds of scuffling from next door, followed by 'terrifying screams ending with a long groan'. She took a stick and knocked on the dividing wall to alert her neighbour on the other side, Mrs Chaplin, who quickly came out into her garden. Mrs Wright said she heard what sounded like men fighting in Busby's house. Mrs Chaplin's mother lived at number 9, next door to Busby on the other side, so she went round to find out if she had heard anything.

Florence Wright stood at her door and watched Mrs Chaplin leave. Three or four minutes later a young man emerged from Busby's house. Mrs Wright shouted 'What are you doing there upsetting people? I shall have a policeman after you!' The man ignored her. He crossed the street, walked past the *Westbury Arms* and disappeared down Ripple Road. Mrs Wright noticed that he was about 5 feet 5 inches tall and wore a brownish tweed cap and a light raincoat with a belt.

PC Leonard Walker was patrolling Ripple Road at about 10.40 p.m. when Mrs Chaplin's husband Harold approached and told him what had happened. Walker came to the house and saw that the front door was slightly ajar, a key in the lock. Mrs Wright confirmed that no one else had come or gone in the meantime. Walker pushed the door, which opened straight into the front room. The light from his torch revealed the figure of Busby lying on his back, feet towards the street door. His right arm was by his side and bent up, and the left arm lay on his chest. The man's head and face were bloodstained. His tongue was protruding, and blood ran from his mouth. There was also a small patch on the linoleum where his head lay. The lower denture of Busby's false teeth was on the floor, while the upper one sat on the footrest of his wheelchair.

PC Walker went across to the *Westbury Arms* to phone for assistance, and by 11.45 p.m. Dr William Fenton and Detective Inspector Hedley Warren were on the scene. The lodger, Albert Harris, had to be awoken by the police. Inspector Warren searched Busby's pockets and found 14s 6d in loose change. An empty wallet lay on the table. Dr Fenton, suspecting Busby had been strangled, asked Warren to cut Busby's shirt, collar and tie away by inserting a knife at the side of his neck.

Meanwhile, Walter Cross's 18 year old wife was asleep at their Orchard Avenue home when he came in just before 10 p.m. They had argued about money earlier that evening. The National Health Service had not yet been set up, and the couple needed to find over £11 in maternity home fees for the birth of their baby in February. Also, Mrs Cross's parents charged them rent of £2 per week but, since leaving his job on 10 October, Cross had received only one week's unemployment benefit, amounting to 31 shillings. Cross had stormed out a couple of hours before, saying he was off to 'see his mate'. Now he woke her up and said he had some money for her, explaining that he had won £20 in a football pools syndicate at his previous place of work. The following morning, Saturday, Cross ordered a cot from the John Edwards shop in the Heathway, to be delivered on Monday. After lunch the young couple took a bus to Romford, buying draperies in British Home Stores and socks in the market. They then returned to the Heathway to buy some nightdresses. They also chose baby clothes and nappies.

Meanwhile, at 12 noon, pathologist Dr F.E. Camps began a post-mortem on the body of Percy Busby at Barking Mortuary. He saw that Busby's legs were very thin and wasted, and the left leg was one and a half inches shorter than the right. His legs, arms and chest were covered with tattoos. Dr Camps found that Busby was suffering from an (unspecified) disease that might eventually have proved fatal, 'and would not therefore be so hard to kill as a normal healthy person'. The cause of death, however, was asphyxia through manual strangulation. Busby had also suffered two blows to the face.

Detectives began the murder investigation by trying to trace Busby's numerous social and business acquaintances. On Saturday morning a policeman stationed outside Busby's house spotted someone walking across the road towards him. The man said his name was Leslie Bull and he'd come to see Busby about a clock for a neighbour in Levine Gardens. The officer told Bull that Busby had been murdered, and that he was directing all visitors to the house to Barking Police Station in Ripple Road for interview. Bull accordingly presented himself before Detective Inspector George Bellamy. Bull explained he had last seen Busby on Wednesday, when he had sold him the shirt and tablecloth. Bellamy noted that Bull, who was about six feet tall, didn't match the description of the man Mrs Wright had seen leaving Busby's home, and allowed him to go.

A modern view of Barking Police Station, where Cross and Bull were questioned. Authors' collection

Soon afterwards, Mrs Rachel Holt was ushered into the Inspector's office. She told him how she had called to see Busby a few days previously and had found two men there whom she didn't know. When Mrs Holt described the tall man who had opened the door to her, Bellamy was sure it must be Leslie Bull. His companion, according to Mrs Holt, had been about 5 feet 5 inches with dark hair brushed back. She said this man 'had what I would call a solemn face and was very quiet'.

On hearing this, Bellamy sent officers out to find Bull again and, at 2 p.m., they returned with him.

'You didn't tell me you were with another man when you called to see Mr Busby', said Bellamy.

'That's right, I didn't', was the reply.

'Why not?'

'I didn't think it was important.'

'I am investigating a case of murder', said Bellamy sternly, 'and it is *essential* that you tell me everything you know. Who was it?'

'I only know him as Ginger Cross', answered Bull, 'but he's all right. He had nothing to do with it.'

He told the Inspector that he had not seen Cross since their visit to Busby's house on Wednesday. Bellamy asked Bull to give him Cross's address, and then allowed him to go home.

Back at Orchard Road, Cross and his wife had not long returned from their shopping trip when Bellamy and another plain clothes officer called to take him to the interview room at the police station. Cross readily admitted going to Busby's house with Bull on two occasions. Bellamy then said 'It was raining last night. Were you wearing a raincoat?'

'No, I haven't got one' replied Cross.

Bellamy noticed that Cross had scratches on his face and left hand. How had he got them?

'Our cat scratched me about a week ago. It fights.'

Cross was then asked what he'd been doing between 8 p.m. and 10 p.m. the previous evening, and replied that he had gone to Leslie Bull's house at 7.30 p.m. Bellamy asked Cross to sign his statement, and then told him he could leave.

Bellamy had, of course, remembered that Bull had said the pair hadn't met since visiting Busby's house on Wednesday. A car was sent to fetch him back to the interview room for the third time that day. 'I have reason to believe you saw Cross again last night', Bellamy began. Bull at first denied it, but when pressed he admitted that Cross had called at his house. On being told he would be detained in custody, Bull became agitated. He screamed 'I didn't do it, I wasn't there, I never meant to do it, Ginger went by himself, I know he did because I gave him the fare to go!'

Bull went on to make a lengthy statement, taking care to play down his own role. He told Bellamy that on leaving Busby's house on Wednesday, Cross had said 'Did you see that money he's got? He hasn't half got a wad there. I could do with it'. The pair had then discussed various methods of robbing Busby, with Cross suggesting 'I'll hide in the front room and when he goes to bed I'll take his trousers with the wallet in'. They had agreed to meet on the Friday evening at the *Chequers* pub before going on to 'do the job'. Bull stayed at home, however, and an angry Cross knocked at his door at about 8 p.m. raging 'I've been waiting a f__ half-hour for you!' Bull said he couldn't leave as he had visitors, and ushered Cross into the scullery. Cross was determined to go alone if necessary, and asked Bull if he had a skeleton key. Bull said he hadn't, and Cross had apparently replied 'One of your keys fits every door in your house, I'll have that', taking the back door key. Bull stated he then gave Cross sixpence for his bus fare.

According to his statement, Bull was getting off a bus outside the *Chequers* the following morning when he bumped into Cross. Bull asked 'Did you go there last night?' and Cross replied 'No, my brother won some money on a fight and lent me £5'. Bull answered 'Thank Christ for that', but privately thought Cross looked 'jittery' and must have been lying. Bull then told Bellamy he had gone to King Edward's Road that morning to satisfy himself that Busby was all right. He said:

The Chequers *pub, where Cross and Bull had planned to meet before the robbery.* LBBD Archives at Valence House Museum

I was afraid of Ginger and although I led him to believe I would help him to get the old man's money, I never intended to. I was really afraid that if he knew I did not intend to help him he would come to my house and do me some injury as he is violent. If you had not sent for me tonight, I should have come here and told you because I could not have stood it any longer.

Cross, in the meantime, had returned home from the police station, not telling his wife the reason he had been questioned. After tea they spent the evening at the nearby Grange Cinema in Goresbrook Road, which was showing *Bachelor Knight*, starring Cary Grant, Myrna Loy and Shirley Temple. Ironically, the supporting feature was entitled *Key Witness*. On leaving at about 9.30 p.m. they found Detective Sergeants Horace Tresidder and John Morton waiting for them. Cross was then driven back to Barking to face George Bellamy once more. 'I have sent for you', began the Inspector, 'because there are one or two points not quite clear.'

The first topic was the raincoat. Cross admitted he had lied about not possessing one. Bellamy then asked 'When you went to see Mr Busby with Bull, did you see his wallet and money?'

'Yes, I did', answered Cross.

'Was anything said about it?'

Under skilful interrogation Cross eventually revealed the whole story, but presented Bull as the prime mover:

Yes, Bull told me the old man was a bit deaf and wouldn't hear us get in if we picked a night when his lodger was at work. He told me we could easily shove him over and get the dough. We were both short of money, so we said we'd do him together. Another thing we thought about was for Bull to go in, start talking to the old man, wave his arms about and break the gas mantle in the kitchen. He would offer to go out and buy a new one, I would then grab the old man and get the loot. He could not go at the last minute, so I went.

Cross described other crimes the pair had planned, including a break-in at the Stadium Café at Dagenham. He told Bellamy that 'I regarded Bull as a man who would use violence on a job because he showed a razor he carried, like an open razor blade without the usual handle, stuck into a small red handle'. Bull, he claimed, had a wooden cosh the size of a chair leg, filled with lead. He had taken it on an intended raid on a petrol station in Gale Street:

He told me he was going into the garage, hit the woman and have the takings. I know he went with the cosh, because I was waiting for him 150 yards away. He came out and said he couldn't do the job because she didn't come out into the office.

Detectives later found a chair leg and razor at Bull's house matching this description.

Meanwhile, Tresidder and Morton had gone to Orchard Avenue and entered Cross's bedroom. A raincoat, still damp, was hanging behind the door. Under a pillow the detectives found fourteen £1 notes and three 10s notes. They returned to the police station and, on entering the room where Cross was being questioned, announced 'Here is £15 10s we found in his bed'. Cross said 'That's right. It is some of the money I took from the old 'un before I slung the wallet'.

Told he would be arrested on suspicion of murder, Cross said 'All right. But I don't remember hitting him'. On being shown his statement, he answered 'I'm not signing it until I know Bull takes his share of the blame'. Bellamy told him that Bull had also been detained and was being interviewed. 'OK then', said Cross, 'I'll sign it'. At 12.50 a.m. on Sunday, after three hours of questioning, Cross was formally charged. He maintained that it was 'all Bull's fault. He put the job up to me and we were going to share the money. He said we would get £150'.

Cross then claimed that on giving him the key, Bull had said 'I put the lock on Busby's door and that should fit it'. Cross described what happened after he entered the house:

I put the key in Busby's door and when it opened I went in and saw Busby coming towards me from the other room. He just hollered, I didn't say anything. He collapsed on the floor and I caught hold of him by the chest and took his wallet from the pocket of his trousers and saw it had a roll of notes in it. I took the notes from the wallet and threw the wallet away. When I left the old man on the floor I thought he had just passed out.

Cross stated that on leaving the house he had run in the direction of Rippleside Cemetery. 'As I was passing the cemetery, I noticed that I had some blood on my little finger of my left hand. I wiped it on some grass.' He bought some cigarettes using one of the notes, then made his way to the *Chequers*, where he had arranged to meet Bull. Not seeing Bull there, he went home. Bellamy asked Cross to take off his jacket, and saw he was wearing a white scarf which appeared to be bloodstained. 'Yes, I wore that last night', volunteered Cross. 'You'll see some [blood] on the raincoat too.'

Dr Fenton took samples of blood from underneath Cross's fingernails, and sent them with the scarf and raincoat to the Hendon Police Laboratory for analysis. They proved to be blood group A, the same as Busby's.

The inquest on Percy Busby opened at East Ham Town Hall on Tuesday, 18 November. His body was formally identified by his brother John, a furniture remover from Upper Norwood. John Busby said they had last met at Finchley Hospital during the First World War, nearly thirty years previously. He declined to take any of his brother's belongings or arrange the funeral.

Cross was sent to Brixton Prison awaiting his appearance before the Stratford magistrates. Detectives had to decide whether Leslie Bull would also face charges. The key found in Busby's front door did also fit the back door of Bull's house, as Cross had told them it would. They noted their belief that 'morally Bull was entitled to stand in the dock with Cross'. After discussions with the Department of Public Prosecutions, however, it became apparent that Bull could not be charged in connection with the death of Busby, and it was decided to call him as a witness for the prosecution.

When Cross was first brought into Stratford Magistrates' Court, reporters noted that he was 'smartly dressed in a dark blue pinstriped suit with a white shirt and neatly placed coloured tie'. After several adjournments, proceedings came to a close on Monday, 8 December. Cross only admitted robbery. He continued to maintain that he didn't assault Busby, but that the man had collapsed in front of him. Dr Camps, who had carried out the post-mortem, was cross-examined by the defence barrister. Camps agreed that Busby might indeed have collapsed and died at any minute, but had definitely been strangled. 'There was no doubt', he declared, 'that the measure of strangulation was sufficient to kill a normal person.' Finally, the magistrates committed Cross for trial at the Old Bailey in the New Year.

Christmas 1947 came and went, and in January the Barking police were surprised to receive a letter from a Mrs E.A. Steers of Detroit, USA, who proved to be Busby's sister. She wrote:

Could you please find out about my brother for me, I am very worried about him…I have sent three boxes of food to him of late, but do not hear if he got them, and as a rule he lets me know when he gets them. I am afraid he is not able to let me know, so if you could let me know about him I will pay for your trouble.

Another brother, Arthur, was traced in Newington, Ontario.

On Wednesday, 14 January the trial got under way. The prosecution put

Leslie Bull in the witness box, but according to police 'his conduct amounted almost to that of a hostile witness'. Bull refused to confirm the statements he had signed at the police station. When the defence counsel, Richard O'Sullivan KC, said 'Cross alleges that you made certain suggestions – how he could get money easily from Busby', Bull flatly denied it.

'Busby was a good friend of mine', he declared.

'It is suggested', continued Mr O'Sullivan, 'that the key found in the front door at the dead man's house came from your back door, and that you knew your key would fit his lock.'

Bull replied 'That is not true. I have never seen that key before'.

After an hour's cross-examination, dramatic scenes occurred when Bull fainted in the witness-box. Three members of the jury rushed to his aid, and the proceedings halted for a few minutes until he had recovered.

The following day, Thursday, Cross himself was called to give evidence. Asked to describe what happened when he entered the house, he said:

> *Busby was kneeling against a marble-topped table. When he saw me he let go of the table and fell, and I shone a torch on him. I saw his wallet sticking out of his trousers pocket. I leaned over and took the wallet and took some of the notes, and threw the rest on the table and went out.*

He denied ever striking or touching Busby at all, and said the time had been only 8.10 p.m. when he left the house. For the defence, Mr O'Sullivan, addressing the jury, suggested that the noises had occurred a considerable time after Cross had left, and that someone else might have entered and committed the murder.

The following day, Friday, 16 January, the jury spent an hour considering their verdict. When they eventually filed back into court, the foreman announced that they found Cross guilty, but that they recommended him to mercy. The judge, Mr Justice Cassels, then pronounced the mandatory sentence of death by hanging. Cross listened without showing any emotion. His teenage wife, however, who had been waiting outside, became hysterical. Screaming, she rushed towards the court, as if attempting to reach her husband. Her cries could still be heard long after Cross had been driven away to the condemned cell at Pentonville Prison.

Cross's legal team launched an appeal, but on Monday, 3 February it was dismissed. They then approached the Home Secretary with a view to having the sentence commuted to a term of imprisonment, as

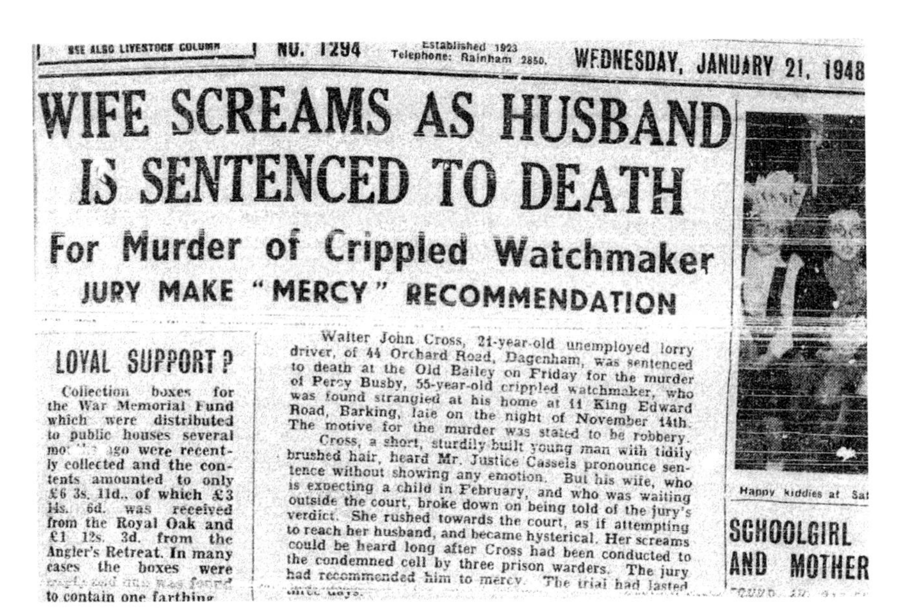

SEE ALSO LIVESTOCK COLUMN | NO. 1294 | Established 1923 Telephone: Rainham 2850. | WEDNESDAY, JANUARY 21, 1948

WIFE SCREAMS AS HUSBAND IS SENTENCED TO DEATH

For Murder of Crippled Watchmaker

JURY MAKE "MERCY" RECOMMENDATION

Walter John Cross, 21-year-old unemployed lorry driver, of 44 Orchard Road, Dagenham, was sentenced to death at the Old Bailey on Friday for the murder of Percy Busby, 55-year-old crippled watchmaker, who was found strangled at his home at 11 King Edward Road, Barking, late on the night of November 14th. The motive for the murder was stated to be robbery.

Cross, a short, sturdily built young man with tidily brushed hair, heard Mr. Justice Cassels pronounce sentence without showing any emotion. But his wife, who is expecting a child in February, and who was waiting outside the court, broke down on being told of the jury's verdict. She rushed towards the court, as if attempting to reach her husband, and became hysterical. Her screams could be heard long after Cross had been conducted to the condemned cell by three prison warders. The jury had recommended him to mercy. The trial had lasted three days.

LOYAL SUPPORT?

Collection boxes for the War Memorial Fund which were distributed to public houses several months ago were recently collected and the contents amounted to only £6 3s. 11d., of which £3 11s. 6d. was received from the Royal Oak and £1 12s. 3d. from the Angler's Retreat. In many cases the boxes were empty and one was found to contain one farthing

Happy kiddies at Sat

SCHOOLGIRL AND MOTHER

The trial verdict is announced. Dagenham Post

recommended by the jury. On 14 February, however, a letter came from the Home Office stating that the Secretary of State had 'failed to discover any sufficient ground to justify him in advising His Majesty to interfere with the course of the law'. Early in the morning ofThursday, 19 February 1948 Cross left his cell at Pentonville and was escorted to the gallows.

Two months later, the House of Commons narrowly voted to abolish the death penalty for murder for a trial period of five years. For a while it looked as though Cross might go down in history as the last person ever to be executed for murder in Britain. Before the end of 1948, however, the decision had been reversed, and executions continued until 1964.

Sources

Depositions (National Archives, MEPO 3/2863)
The *Dagenham Post*
The *Barking Advertiser*

Chapter 21

The Ilford Kid 1956

He had approached silently, then whipped out an axe from beneath his coat...

In the early hours of 29 July 1948 Alfred Roome, known to London's underworld as the Ilford Kid, placed a key in the door of a safe within a Customs shed at Heathrow Airport. It was the culmination of many months of careful planning by Roome and his accomplices, for within the safe was a haul of South African diamonds, and nearby lay gold bullion and other valuables worth over a quarter of a million pounds.

Suddenly he heard a shout. 'We are police of the Flying Squad – stand where you are!' Roome spun round and saw figures dressed as security guards, porters and clerks. The police had clearly been tipped off about the raid and lain in wait. Roome and his gang did not go quietly, however. They fought for an hour with weighted sticks and bottles in what became known as the Battle of London Airport. The would-be robbers were eventually captured and sent for trial. Roome, said to be a ringleader, was alleged to have swung an iron bar at an officer's head, which could well have proved fatal had it made contact. He was sentenced to ten years' imprisonment.

In the summer of 1955 Roome, then 49, was released to return to his wife, Sarah Elizabeth, at Bath Road in Chadwell Heath. For the past three years Mrs Roome had worked at a newspaper stand outside the Ford motor

New Road, Dagenham, showing the entrance to Ford's on the left. LBBD Archives at Valence House Museum

factory in order to support herself and her two children. The stand was run by 42 year old Joseph Winch, a former lightweight professional boxer whose mother owned a grocer's shop in Crown Street, Dagenham Village.

Alfred Roome's return soon proved a nightmare for his wife. She only had to speak to another man for Roome to accuse her of being unfaithful. He was also prone to violence. Sarah remembered that 'He assaulted me frequently. He beat me until I was unconscious, and then he seemed to be sorry afterwards. He used to say something came over him.' Roome occasionally helped serve at the newspaper stand, but disapproved of Sarah working there, saying 'it was the type of job *he* should have'. He ordered Joseph Winch to stop employing her, but without success.

Winch often collected Sarah in his car to take her to work, and inevitably the pathologically jealous Roome convinced himself they were having an affair. The final straw for Sarah was when her husband threatened to take the younger child away from her. She later described how 'I told him I wouldn't live with him again and he said I would suffer and he would do me some injury'. Sarah took legal advice, and in early January 1956 she was granted an official separation order. She moved to St Chad's Road, also in Chadwell Heath, while her husband went to stay with a sister in Chandos Road, Stratford.

Roome then took out his anger on his elder child 21 year old Sheila. She was shortly to be married, and in a fit of rage he burned her clothes, but she just managed to save her wedding dress. As a result of this, Roome was summoned to Stratford Magistrates' Court on Wednesday, 18 January accused of malicious damage. Sheila's wedding was to take place at noon on the Saturday, three days later, but it was decided to bring it forward to 11 a.m. in case Roome tried to cause further trouble.

On the afternoon of Thursday, 19 January, the day following Roome's court appearance, Joseph Winch and Sarah Roome were selling their papers as usual outside Ford's. They expected a rush in trade when the workers of the main shift left the factory in a few minutes' time. Sarah suddenly became aware of someone behind her. She remembered that 'I looked up and all I could see was a man's hand coming down...The hand came down on my left where Mr Winch was standing'. The figure was Alfred Roome. He had approached silently, then whipped out an axe from beneath his coat and struck Joseph Winch on the head. Winch fell to the ground, blood pouring from his skull.

Sarah:

...saw the man's face but didn't recognise my husband because the face was discoloured. I just stood for a minute and then I ran. I ran towards the road

Dagenham Post

AND CHADWELL HEATH NEWS

Telephone: Dominion 2267/8

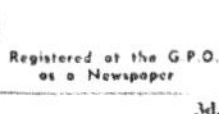

Registered at the G.P.O. as a Newspaper

No. 1711 WEDNESDAY, JANUARY 25, 1956 3d.

HATCHET ATTACK: FULL STORY

The scene of the attack. The arrow points to the newspaper stall where Mr. Winch was working with Mrs. Roome before he was struck down. Security police on duty at the main gates rushed to their aid and carried them and Mr. Roome into their lodge.
Photo: Springer, Ilford

DRAMA OUTSIDE FORD'S

Was jealousy motive of ex-convict's assault?

JEALOUSY is believed to be the motive that drove ex-jailbird 49-year-old Alfred Roome to savagely attack newspaper seller Joseph Winch and then take his own life by drinking poison . . . .

Pictures of the year display

IN conjunction with Mr. E. C. Carter, manager of the Gaumont Cinema, Heathway, this paper is sponsoring an exhibition of news photographs to be held in the upstairs foyer

P.C. beaten up: Man remanded

A DAGENHAM police constable was beaten up in Wood Lane on Thursday night and his leg was broken in the attack. As a result at Stratford Court on Monday, Frederick John Cooper, aged 27, a coalman, of Hat & Sutlons Hostel, Hornchurch, was remanded in custody until January 30.

Dramatic headlines followed the attempted murders outside Ford's. Dagenham Post

and looked back and saw it was my husband. He was running after me.

Roome caught up with his wife, grabbed hold of her and pulled an open razor out of his pocket. He turned Sarah round and lunged at her with the blade. 'I struggled and pulled my coat over my face. He was slashing at me.' She managed to seize the razor from him, severely wounding her own hand as she did so.

Meanwhile, Ford security officers had seen the scuffle from their lodge at the factory gates, and ran to the scene. One of them, Ronald Scott, caught hold of Roome's arm and dragged him away. He noticed that the attacker was holding a bottle, which fell to the ground and shattered. Scott reported that 'He turned round to me and said "You are too late". He looked in a very bad way'. The men were setting off with Roome back to the security lodge when he suddenly collapsed. Scott remembered that 'He looked very poorly – on the point of dying. His face was very blue and I thought he had gone into a fit'. Within seconds Roome had stopped breathing. The bottle had contained deadly potassium cyanide, which he drank immediately before attacking Winch with the axe. Roome's victims were rushed to Oldchurch Hospital in Romford. Joseph Winch had suffered a fractured skull, but was soon reported to be 'out of danger and likely to recover'.

Two days after the attack, police officers stood outside St Chad's Church as guests arrived for the wedding of Sheila Roome. She and her mother were now living opposite the church, and as the clock struck eleven Mrs Roome emerged from the house, dressed in sombre grey and with an arm in a black sling. She had to be helped across the road. A few minutes later the bride appeared, wearing a gown of white lace. Mrs Roome left the church before the end of the service and returned home, onlookers noting that she 'appeared to be in a state of collapse'. The newlyweds attempted to pose outside the main doors of the church for their official photographs, but chaos ensued as they were mobbed by press photographers and reporters. Wedding guests shouted at them to go away, and crowded around the couple in an attempt to shield them from the intrusion.

A modern view of St Chad's Church, where the press converged for the wedding of Alfred Roome's daughter, causing chaotic scenes. Authors' collection

Meanwhile, detectives had discovered that Roome had purchased both the axe and the razor just hours before the attack. On going to the house in Stratford where he had lodged, they found another bottle of cyanide in his bedside cabinet, wrapped in old newspaper. A pathologist told the inquest that Roome had taken more than five times the fatal dose. He was hurriedly buried in an unmarked grave at West Ham Cemetery.

Sources

The Times
The *Dagenham Post*

Bibliography

Clifford, Tony: *Barking & Dagenham buildings past and present* (LBBD. 1992) – *Dagenham Pubs Past & Present* (LBBD. 1993)

Gwilliam, Peter: *Old Chadwell Heath* (St Chad's Parochial Church Council, 1983)

Hewson, Don: *Chadwell Heath and the Road to Romford Market* (Alan Sutton, 1995)

Shawcross, John Peter: *A History of Dagenham in the County of Essex* (Skeffington & Son, 2nd edition 1908)

Old Ordnance Survey maps: *Creekmouth 1894; Chadwell Heath 1914*; and *Goodmayes & Seven Kings 1915* (reprinted by Alan Godfrey Publications)

Other sources are given at the end of each chapter.

Index